Four Di:
Questions
Simple Answer

Also by Tim Sledge

Making Peace with Your Past (1992)

Moving Beyond Your Past (1994)

Goodbye Jesus: An Evangelical Preacher's Journey Beyond Faith (2018)

How to Live a Meaningful Life: Focusing on Things that Matter (2019)

You can contact Tim Sledge on his website, MovingTruths.com, where he shares insights for personal growth.

Follow Tim Sledge on Twitter: https://twitter.com/Goodbye_Jesus

Four Disturbing Questions with One Simple Answer

Breaking the Spell of Christian Belief

Tim Sledge

About the Author

Tim Sledge is a humanist writer and speaker whose mission is discovering and sharing insights for personal growth. You can read his latest articles and stay in touch via his website, MovingTruths.com.

Sledge is a former Southern Baptist pastor and author. After devoting his career as an evangelical preacher to leading and growing ministries in Illinois, Tennessee, New Jersey, and Arizona, he moved to a suburb of Houston, Texas, where, as senior pastor, he led his church to experience dramatic growth and wrote two books that launched a ground-breaking support group ministry. *Making Peace with Your Past* and *Moving Beyond Your Past* have now been in print for more than 25 years, and have been used as interactive guides for 20,000 support groups across the U.S.

At the peak of his ministerial career, a 10-year series of events led to a growing awareness that faith was no longer working for him. His journey into and out of faith is described in *Goodbye Jesus: An Evangelical Preacher's Journey Beyond Faith*.

Contents

Introduction

In fairy tales some unfortunate person may be the victim of a magic spell. A handsome prince can be turned into an ugly beast. A beautiful young woman can be sentenced to a 100-year-long snooze. Tales of magic abound in stories of all kinds. A magic spell might immobilize you or make you do something you don't want to do. A spell might silence you or make you say things you would never choose to say.

In the world of storytelling, spells that trap you in some state from which you urgently want to escape are scary. But the most frightening type of spell would be one that orders your thoughts, words, and behaviors while making it seem that you're acting freely—a spell that controls without your being aware of it.

I don't believe in magic, but I lived under a trancelike spell for five decades. I wasn't turned into a frog or put to sleep. I felt wide awake and saw myself as fully functional, reaching for all life had to offer me. Nevertheless, I was under a spell that shaped my thinking and guided my actions.

The spell was Christian faith. In my view, it was something I chose freely, but it started when I was an impressionable nine years old. And I chose it because adults told me that believing in Jesus was what good boys do and if I didn't choose Jesus, I would go to hell.

I devoted my life to this magic spell, and as a Christian minister I did all I could to cast the spell on anyone who would permit me to do so.

In fairy tales, there's usually a way to break the spell, like a kiss from a prince or princess. When it comes to breaking the spell of a lifelong belief system, a jolt may be required—some experience of loss or pain, some type of wakeup call. That's what happened to me. Multiple jolts stirred me from my trancelike state.

After a series of losses, failures, and other emotionally painful events, the trance of belief began to lose its grip. I was slowly waking up and gradually realizing that part of me had been locked in a small thought prison since childhood. I began to learn how to think without fences around forbidden zones where truth might reside. And a multitude of things that had made perfect sense began to look patently foolish.

Eventually, the spell was completely broken.

I've shared the details of my spiritual journey in *Goodbye Jesus: An Evangelical Preacher's Journey Beyond Faith*. My aim in this book is to cut to the chase by raising four challenging questions for Christian believers and then sharing what I consider the one incredibly simple answer—an answer not only to my four questions but to many kindred questions concerning faith and religion.

Even if life has jostled you in some way that has made you question your faith—you may find this book disturbing, disconcerting, and unnerving. During the early stages of waking up from my faith, I started reading a book that challenged the idea that a loving God could send people to burn in hell for eternity. What I read made perfect sense, but I did not feel free to adopt the view espoused by the authors, and I stopped reading the book. It was too threatening.

So, if you feel some ambivalence, I understand.

Leaving a closely held belief system is not a walk in the park. And facing up to the idea that you might be under a spell that makes it hard for you to think objectively is daunting, especially when you rely on the spell's results to make you feel that everything's okay and when you've been warned that tampering with the spell is the worst thing you could ever do.

Choose courage. If what you believe is true, it can stand the test of any question that I or anyone else might raise. I encourage you to open your mind, face the facts, and to decide that you will follow the truth wherever it leads. I spent most of my life in a search for truth about faith, God, and religion. Maybe I can save you some time as you make your own decisions.

Tim Sledge

1 – The Power Failure Question

Starting out as a teenage Baptist preacher in West Texas, my ears perked up whenever I heard someone say, "All religions are basically the same." I saw Christianity as the one true faith, so I automatically rejected the notion that all religions could be the same. But I didn't know enough about any belief system other than my own to effectively defend my opinion.

I was surprised at how little attention was paid to the study of other faiths in my Christian college and seminary studies, but I did learn that the differences in the world's religions are so plentiful that it's hard to keep up with all the distinctions. I discovered diverse views of deity and different ideas on how to discover ultimate spiritual truth.

I did note superficial similarities like calling adherents to worship and prayer, and I learned that some faiths share common roots. But I found significant variations in each religion's description of the most important things to know and do as well as divergent beliefs about what happens after death.

It didn't take a lot of study to decide that anyone who says all religions are basically the same doesn't know much about religion.

By the time I received my seminary doctorate, I was even more confident regarding the distinctiveness of my Christian faith, and I was well equipped to counter anyone's assertion that all religions are fundamentally alike. I saw all faiths other than Christianity as human attempts to find God, but in Jesus, God revealed himself to humanity and offered the strength to live a changed life.

I learned the theological terms used to describe different aspects of what happens when an individual makes a faith-driven, once-in-a-lifetime commitment to Jesus—words like justification, regeneration, and salvation. But no matter what theological jargon was used to explain the experience, the anticipated result was not in question: Giving your life to Jesus would change you so dramatically that it would be appropriate to describe the experience as being born again.

But in the following decades of my life as a minister, I did observe one clear, undeniable, and surprising characteristic of Christianity that it shares with all other religions: *Some followers of Jesus are far more committed than others.*

If you're a Christian, you may argue that your brand of Christianity works better than any other. But I'm confident that your version of following Jesus—whatever it might look like—has not only some dedicated devotees, but also significant numbers of lukewarm believers, and many who are followers in name only. I'm certain that your local flock includes a small segment of fervent folks who give as much of their time, energy, and effort as they can and another group who may or may not show up for services on any given week.

All faiths are alike in this respect. Each has a significant number of casual adherents. No religion produces only unswerving believers.

In my preaching, I never stopped declaring that the Christian faith is different from all the rest—not just a human effort to obey God, but rather, a source of divine power for a new way of living. But I found that the results of Christian conversion were not as predictable as one would expect from an empowering personal encounter with God. Sometimes a decision to follow Jesus led to significant life changes, but often, it did not.

During my fresh-out-of-seminary pastorate in a suburb of New York City, one of my newest converts robbed a bank and went to prison. This was deeply unsettling and certainly not how faith was supposed to work. But my theological training had prepared me for such disappointments by equipping me with an array of answers as to why faith in Jesus can produce uneven results.

I was taught that sometimes the seed of God's message falls on fertile ground. This is what happens when a person who sincerely believes and is willing to change responds to the gospel message. This is when salvation works.

At other times the seed of the gospel message falls on rocky ground: The individual goes through the motions of beginning the Christian life, but the tree of belief develops no roots. For a short period, the individual's new commitment looks like real faith, but when trouble or persecution comes they walk away.

And sometimes a new commitment to follow Jesus makes it out of the starting gate but gets bogged down by the cares and temptations of the world and drops out. Not an overnight failure, but still another instance where something that looks like sincere belief really isn't.[1]

It is a kind of circular logic: If conversion leads to positive, significant, and lasting changes in a life, then it's genuine faith at work. If the commitment doesn't last or doesn't lead to a changed life, the "faith" isn't real faith.

But questions about how much difference faith makes weren't just raised by new believers. Too often it was hard to see significant faith results in the lives of individuals who had been Christians for decades—individuals who showed up to study the Bible and worship Sunday after Sunday. Many of these long-term believers displayed little evidence of spiritual growth and could be blatantly hypocritical.

My theological education had prepared me to face this apparent inconsistency as well. I understood that a commitment to Jesus was just the beginning of a lifelong growth process that requires multiple disciplines including Bible study, prayer, worship, ministry to others, and financial giving. I believed that if you didn't practice these disciplines, you wouldn't grow in your faith, and your life might not look much different than a non-believer's life.

I came to understand that Christians need constant exhortation and encouragement to live as disciples— followers of Jesus who keep learning and doing the things that lead to continual spiritual growth.

If someone from another religion indicated their faith wasn't working, in my view, the problem was the religion. As the one true religion, Christianity was the only kind of faith that could be expected to actually work. But if a Christian's faith was dysfunctional, the problem wasn't Christianity. The problem was with the believer.

Spiritual trouble-shooting for a troubled Christian would begin with this question: "Did you ever come to one specific point in your life when you sincerely and wholeheartedly accepted Jesus as your personal lord and savior?" In other words, "Are you really a Christian?"

This line of questioning grew out of the concern that the individual—though having gone through the outward motions of accepting Jesus—had, at some private level failed to truly confess or fully commit to Jesus. Such a person was still in need of a born-again conversion experience—church member or not.

As a minister, I would often assist individuals in reviewing their first steps in Christian belief to help them ascertain whether their faith in Jesus was authentic.

I re-baptized many individuals in my years of ministry. These were people who decided their initial experience with Jesus was not valid, prayed again to receive him— this time the "right" way—and then requested a new, now valid baptism.

Another aspect of this type of spiritual review would be determining whether the individual was involved with a Bible-believing church. You could not expect a meaningful spiritual life if you were participating in a church that was teaching a distorted version of Christianity.

Once the issues of how faith had begun and whether one was in the right church were settled, the next step was determining whether the believer was out of fellowship with God.

You could be a true believer who had gotten out of step with God because of disobedience, lack of prayer, poor church attendance, or any one of a million other ways. So, if a Christian was acting badly, s/he might be temporarily out of fellowship with God, and a series of reflective questions were in order.

Is there some sin that needs to be confessed and removed? Is it time to get rid of a bad habit that keeps me from being more Christlike? Am I praying enough? Am I devoted enough to studying the Bible? Am I contributing enough of my time and money? Do I need to forgive someone?

The idea was to look for some area where commitment could be stronger. You prayed for guidance, and when you found a problem area, you asked for forgiveness, resolved to correct the errant behavior, and stepped back onto the pathway of more consistent obedience.

Over the course of a Christian life, this process of soul searching would be repeated many times. Your task was to keep moving up the ladder of spiritual growth.

But years of being challenged to climb this spiritual ladder coupled with decades of church attendance, worship, prayer, and Bible study often seemed to have little impact on the most challenging issues faced by Christians.

As one individual who gave it her all explained:

> What I found to be true was that "old things" had NOT passed away and "all things" had NOT become new. It was the same old, same old. Unless, of course, I pretended and continued with a fake smile!

I consistently observed believers who could not escape the grip of compulsive behaviors ranging from bad habits to substance addictions. And I noted that sincere Christians could be chronically troubled by the after-effects of growing up in a dysfunctional family. Ironically, some of the most committed believers I knew—including ministers—were living with unrelenting emotional pain.

And I was surprised at how often the values and decisions of believers were shaped more by cultural norms than by any spiritual transformation.

As a youth minister in Memphis, Tennessee, while a seminary student, I watched the deacons in the inner-city church I served respond to a threatened protest by the NAACP. The church had refused to admit an African American girl to its weekday preschool. In the deacons meeting, there was no discussion of changing the preschool's admissions policy. There was no conversation about Jesus's teachings on loving and accepting all people.

No one pulled out his Bible for guidance that day. The response of the deacons—the most respected lay leaders in our church—was driven by long-standing racial prejudice ingrained in Southern culture.

The deacons' discussion would have made more sense if someone had opened a Bible. One of the foundational pillars of the Christian faith is the assertion that the Bible is the record of God's revelation of himself to humanity. As far as Christian believers are concerned, the Bible contains the answers to life's most significant questions and is the most important book in the world.

It would then seem to be a safe assumption that Christians

place the highest priority on reading the Bible from cover-to-cover—not once but many times. Surprisingly, that's not the case. While around 70% of Americans claim to be Christians, only about 20% have read the entire Bible even one time.[2]

This level of interest in Bible reading and study was validated in each congregation I served. For many Christians, the Bible is revered but seldom read.

One thing is crystal clear in the Bible: Jesus expects his followers to take the gospel message to everyone—near and far. After his resurrection, Jesus shared the Great Commission with his disciples:

> Therefore go and make disciples of all nations, baptizing them in the name of the Father and of the Son and of the Holy Spirit, and teaching them to obey everything I have commanded you.[3]

It's easy to make a case that spreading the message of salvation through Jesus is the most important job the church is called to do. But making evangelistic church growth a top priority in a congregation is such a challenging task that it is rarely accomplished.

Most U.S. churches never break the 200 mark in average attendance. There are many reasons for this, but one of the most disconcerting is that congregations are filled with members who see the main role of their pastor and their church as meeting their own personal needs.

One of the most startling and disappointing facts of life for me as a pastor was discovering through experience how hard it is to motivate a church to grow. After 10 years of trying unsuccessfully to inspire and lead two different churches to experience dramatic grow, I moved to a suburb of Houston where I was able to lead the church I pastored to quadruple in size.

In 1990, the Houston church I led was recognized as one of the 540 fastest growing churches out of more than 400,000 congregations in North America. That same year, our church was ranked 225th out of 43,000 Southern Baptist churches in the number of converts baptized. But during our church's ten years of growth, I saw how selfish long-term Christians could be when it comes to holding on to tradition, influence, and power in their own congregation.

For a Christian church, sharing the gospel message and experiencing growth as new converts join should be as natural as flying is for birds—but it isn't. Leading a congregation to look beyond their own needs, to embrace a vision for reaching non-believers, and to assimilate new members into their fold is one of the most challenging leadership tasks faced by a minister.

This unexpected uphill battle raised an uncomfortable question: How could true believers have such difficulty getting beyond lip service to such a basic and important command to share the gospel message with others?

Another substantial challenge is motivating congregants to share their financial resources to support their church's ministries. The theological basis for financial giving is the concept that everything the believer has is a gift from God. When Christians make financial contributions to support the church, they are simply giving back a portion of what God has given to them.

When our Houston congregation hired a fund-raising consultant to help enlist commitments to finance a new worship center, the consultant started with a simple assumption in fashioning our plan for raising money. Before even looking at our contribution records, he knew that a small group—20 to 30 percent of our members— gave 70 or 80 percent of the funds received. He also knew that the differences in giving levels were contoured more by commitment level than by personal income.

The fund-raising consultant could accurately assume these facts because they are the norm for Christian congregations—regardless of size, location, or denomination. A faithful few give most of the money and do most of the work.

But wouldn't it be logical to expect a different standard for a supernaturally powered organization—a dramatically higher percentage of committed, hard-working, involved members than is the norm for any volunteer organization, including secular ones?

Another reason to question the supernatural element in Christian congregations can be seen in the consistent failures of congregations to agree on how God is leading them. A large aspect of prayer is "seeking an answer from the Lord." Born-again believers can talk to God and sense his leadership.

Take a group of these born-again, new creations in Christ—to whom God is giving directions and guidance for day-to-day life—put them in a church and wait. Eventually, some of them will get into a disagreement about something. Sometimes, they work it out, but often, no matter how much prayer takes place, one group gets angry and leaves, often to start another congregation.

Wait a little longer, and the process will repeat—over and over—and that's one reason we have not only thousands of churches, but thousands of Christian denominations.

I had to wonder how individuals who are supposedly connected to the same God—changed by him, talking and listening to him, and using the same book he has provided for guidance—could be so at odds with each other so often?

In each place I served, a higher-than-average number of the people I ministered to were salt of the earth individuals. My life was enriched by the many laypersons who were sincerely committed, worked hard to live out their faith consistently, and were open to helping with whatever God seemed to be leading our church to do.

But as I thought about the range of personalities and lifestyles in any congregation I served or visited, I saw a bell curve of outstanding, average, and not-so-great people not dramatically different from the pattern of any human organization.

Christian faith helps some individuals become better human beings—sometimes great human beings. Some Christians wield significant influence for good. But across the board, the results of believing in Jesus are disappointingly inconsistent.

Christianity claims to be energized by God's supernatural power and promises to connect you as a believer with this supernatural power. It promises to make you a new person and to enable you to bear the fruits of the Spirit: love, joy, peace, patience, goodness, and more. Unfortunately, in real life, the results of faith in Jesus can be hit or miss.

After decades of ministry in up-close relationships with Christians in churches I served in five different regions of the U.S., there was one question I found more and more difficult to ignore:

> **Why does faith in the resurrected,**
> **empowering Jesus generate such**
> **inconsistent results?**

If you had asked me this question while I was still a pastor, my reply would have sounded something like the following:

The reasons for faith's inconsistent results are explained in the Bible. Jesus predicted some would start faith but quickly slip away. Jesus predicted that some who were not true disciples would call him Lord.

True faith begins when you—at one specific point in your life—believe, repent of your sins, and fully commit yourself to Jesus. This is what it means to become a Christian, and it's how you begin a personal relationship with God. And when your decision to follow Jesus is genuine, your faith will preserve no matter what challenges it faces.

One of the reasons the church has survived for centuries is that life-changing conversions do happen. And we can see the results in the genuine supernatural spiritual power at work in the changed lives of committed believers.

Life in the church can be touched by human pride, temptations, and personal weakness. But the humanity of the church is not a reason for unbelief. Churches are imperfect because they are made up of imperfect people who are on a spiritual journey.

The Bible doesn't teach that giving yourself to Jesus will make you sinless—at least not in this life. The Christian life is a process of

> growth that's not done until we get to heaven where the work of our salvation will be completed.
>
> And if your faith seems to be ineffective, it's time to search your heart to see what is holding you back.

I tried to be honest when I didn't have a neat and easy answer, but for this question, there seemed to be plenty of answers, and I attempted to articulate the most faith-building responses I could muster.

My answers were not parroted. They expressed sincere beliefs that enabled me to keep going in my faith even when I couldn't stop asking myself the question:

Why does faith in the resurrected, empowering Jesus generate such inconsistent results?

2 – The Mixed Messages Question

One of the first things you learn in church is that God is uniquely worthy of praise. He is the creator of all that exists. He is all-powerful and all-knowing. God has no beginning or end. No matter where you go, God is there, but he is also beyond the here and now, transcending all that we understand.

Christians see evidence of the creator's power and knowledge everywhere: in the countless galaxies that surround our own Milky Way, in the breathtaking beauty of earth's natural wonders, and in the beautiful complexity of a single human being.

It's a logical assumption that the God tailored with all the attributes described above also possesses communication skills beyond what we can imagine. It would make no sense to think that the God who gave humans the gift of speech could—in any way—be speech impaired.

A God who isn't interested in his creation—though

eminently qualified to communicate—might choose to say nothing. Silence is consistent with a God who doesn't care. But the God of the Bible is not a disinterested deity. A simple statement from the New Testament attempts to sum up his character: God is love. [4] He is not cold and unknowable. This God wants to be known by his creation.

It makes sense that a caring God would have a message for those made in his image. How could a God of love not self-reveal and let people know what he expects?

Regardless of the solid logic behind the idea that a loving creator God would have the desire and unparalleled ability to communicate with us clearly, the reality is: *No God— including the God of the Bible—has self-revealed in a manner that is completely clear and unmistakably true.*

What we have is a confusing array of mixed messages emanating from more than 4,000 religions.

When I was a pastor, I would have responded to this assertion as follows.

> God did not do a poor job of self-revelation! We do have a clear and unmistakably true revelation from God.

> God has clearly revealed himself to humanity in Jesus Christ, and more than two billion people alive today are his followers.

The Bible is the trustworthy, infallible, and complete record of God's revelation of himself to humanity. The heart of the Bible's message is the story of Jesus, the Son of God who became a man, lived a perfect life, died for our sins, and rose from the dead.

By accepting God's plan of salvation so clearly explained in the Bible and made possible by the death of Jesus on the cross, we can be forgiven, live changed lives, and spend eternity with God in heaven instead of suffering in hell.

How can we ignore the timeless relevance of this ancient book which still pierces the hearts of men and women when they hear its true message?

It does take effort to understand the Bible, but it's not an impossible task. With an open mind and the guidance of the Holy Spirit to illuminate the Bible's meaning, anyone can grasp its life-changing message.

All other religions are human attempts to reach up to God. Christianity is God reaching down to humanity and offering forgiveness and spiritual power to live as he wants us to live.

My current response to my old view is this: It's true that

more than two billion people alive today identify with some version of the propositions stated in my former view, but over five billion people don't believe. It's convenient to say the five billion have simply chosen to reject the Christian message, but that's not how it is.

More than any other factor, one's religious "choice" is determined by geography. If you consider the list of religious preferences by country, you will find few nations with a balance of multiple religions. Typically, a country has one predominant faith.

Statistically, you are likely to be linked to the primary belief system of the country or region where you were raised. If you are a person of faith, you're likely to be Buddhist if you live in Cambodia, Hindu if you live in Nepal, Muslim if you live in Egypt, and Christian if you live in the U.S.

If you are from one of a minority of countries where less than 50% of the population is affiliated with one brand of belief, you are still religiously predictable in that you are likely to share the same faith as your parents.

Church growth studies indicate that only a small percentage of adults make radical changes in their religious affiliation. Exceptions occur when cultures experience a major shift in the predominant religion. For instance, while it has taken centuries, Africa has gone from having most of the population as adherents of indigenous, traditional religions, to being predominantly Christian and

Muslim. South Korea, once a shamanistic and Confucian country, now finds its cities dotted with red crosses and produces more Christian missionaries than any country except the U.S.[5]

Another exception occurs when a generational age group moves toward a different view of religion due to a cultural shift. Example: A 2015 article indicated that 36% of Millennials are unaffiliated with any faith—twice the number of unaffiliated Baby Boomers.[6]

Your belief system is likely something you "chose" as a child. Most believers adopt religious faith in the same way they choose their native language—in other words, they don't really choose it. They are born into it, surrounded by it, and likely indoctrinated into it.[7]

A completely clear and unmistakably true message from God wouldn't be determined or deterred by anyone's childhood religious roots. It wouldn't matter where you were born, what your parents taught you, or what belief trends were shaping your generation. A clear message from the creator of all things would be unavoidably powerful, unmistakably unique, and inescapably captivating.

Not only does the Bible fail to meet these criteria for capturing the attention of those who do not believe, it's an incredibly confusing source of information for those who do accept its message.

Have you ever met anyone who told you they started reading the Bible and couldn't put it down? I'm guessing you haven't, and the reason is that the Bible is hard to read, difficult to understand, and filled with contradictions.

If the Bible is in fact God's true revelation of himself to humanity, then he did a remarkably poor job of delivering his message. While it's true that any Christian is likely to have a basic understanding of the idea that Jesus died for our sins and rose again to offer us eternal life, there are countless areas where even Christian theologians cannot agree on what the Bible has to say. Here are 25 examples of things upon which Christians cannot agree. And this is only a shortlist.

1. How do you become a Christian?
2. Can you lose your salvation?
3. Baptism by sprinkling, pouring, or immersion?
4. When do children become accountable for faith?
5. Is Jesus the only way to go to heaven?
6. Will non-believers go to hell?
7. Are we predestined to believe or not believe?
8. How authoritative is the Bible?
9. Does the Bible contain errors?
10. Is the earth thousands or billions of years old?
11. Is Satan a real personal being?
12. Does prayer heal the sick?
13. What is the correct form of church governance?
14. Should Christians speak in unknown tongues?
15. Can clergy be married?
16. Does divorce disqualify for ordained leadership?

17. Is abortion a sin?
18. Can women be ordained to the ministry?
19. Should a pulpit or an altar take center stage?
20. Should wives be submissive to their husbands?
21. Should women wear makeup and jewelry?
22. Does Jesus point you left or right in politics?
23. Is homosexuality sinful?
24. Is premarital sex okay for committed adults?
25. What is the meaning of the book of Revelation?

The existence of tens of thousands of Christian denominations is an inescapable argument against the Bible's clarity. And the confusion generated by the Bible is not the only reason to question its authority.

For Christians, the books of the New Testament are the most recent and most important part of their sourcebook of faith, but no one has the original Greek manuscripts of any these—which is strange given the supposed earth-shattering importance of the message of these writings.

We have more than 5,000 manuscripts containing at least a portion of the Greek New Testament. Only eight of these manuscripts may be as early as the 2nd century, 40 as early as the 3rd century, and more than 80% are from the 11th to 16th centuries. The oldest complete copy of the whole New Testament in Greek dates to sometime in the 4th century.

One more surprising fact: It took hundreds of years for church leaders to agree on which books should be included in the New Testament. The earliest authoritative statement listing the 27 books that make up the New Testament today was included in the annual Easter letter of Athanasius, Bishop of Alexandria, in 367 A.D.

While most of the books of the New Testament had long been acknowledged as authoritative by the time the full list was finalized, some—including the book of Revelation—were still in question.

The 27 books that made the final cut were not the only "inspired" books under consideration. Other Gospels and epistles had been written and needed an official yes or no. Even after the proclamation by Athanasius, some Christian leaders continued to assert that several books left off the list of the 27 approved New Testament books should also be regarded as inspired and authoritative.[8]

The Bible is a source of widespread, conflict-generating, and sometimes life-altering confusion, and it took Christian leaders centuries to finalize its contents. One must ask why this is the case if the Bible is, in fact, God's all-important self-revelation to humanity.

Imagine you are an all-powerful, loving God, and you have created humans in your own image. It is your desire that they know who you are, how much you love them, and what you expect of them. You want every individual who will ever live to know and understand these things.

How would you make yourself known? Whatever plan for

self-disclosure you might devise, I'm sure it would be a better plan than anything in this world that purports to be a revelation from any God—including the Bible and the events it records.

Would you let humans exist for thousands of years before revealing yourself? What purpose would that serve and how could it be fair to the countless individuals whose lives were over before your self-disclosure?

Would you limit your self-revelation to a small group of people you declare to be your chosen ones? Why would you entrust the accurate disclosure of your identity and plans to people who themselves have difficulty in understanding and obeying?

Would you give this all-important task to a group who are not even aware of how many other people exist in your world? Why would you depend on people who—even if they knew the locations and identities of all other nations—were dramatically limited in their ability to travel and to communicate with the rest of humanity?

Why self-reveal in a way that makes your message inaccessible to most people alive at the time you reveal yourself?

Would you rely on a religious book full of erroneous and contradictory ideas about how humans came to exist, how the world works, and how people should live? And would you count on word-of-mouth stories about your visit to earth for decades before anything was written down?

As the creator of all communication skills—with unlimited resources at your disposal—why would you resort to any of these obviously flawed methods?

There would be no reason to utilize any plan so ineffective and confusing that it created thousands of explanations of your identity, character, and guidelines for living. And yet, this is exactly the situation in our world.

Proponents of each religion will assert their God has unambiguously revealed himself. It is the business of each faith to share its unique understanding of how God has "clearly" made himself known.

Whatever your holy book is, you'll need a guide to make sense of it, and that's one of the reasons clergy are required. Religious leaders and teachers go through rigorous training to learn answers to the questions raised by their ancient, authoritative books. And one of the most important is the answer to the question: "Why is your book better than all the rest?"

As science provides more and more evidence about how the universe, our world, our bodies, and especially our brains work, new challenges are generated for ancient religious books. We now understand that the Bible, for example, gets the chronology of creation wrong, asserts that the sun once stopped in its tracks, and hasn't a clue about the age of the earth. It doesn't account for the

Neanderthals, is completely unaware of subconscious thinking, and reflects no meaningful awareness of the causes of human illnesses.

As knowledge increases and shines its light on the inadequacies of authoritative religious books, two options are available for people of faith.

One option is to retreat to a religious fundamentalism that turns a blind eye to modern discoveries and opts to live with an outdated mindset. Fundamentalism generates mind-boggling contradictions like a Texas geologist who works for a big oil company during the week to help them know where to look for oil created by life forms that decomposed millions of years ago and on Sundays attends a church where the pastor claims the earth is 6,000 years old. Fundamentalism creates massive cognitive dissonance that cripples a believer's ability to think clearly about information that contradicts his/her holy book.

The other option for people of faith when science challenges their divine book is to adapt by reinterpreting its sacred writings. It is the task of separating what is no longer true from what is timeless, and this is a chore that must be undertaken over and over.

It's an Edward Scissorhands approach to the Bible: Cut, cut, cut until you have something presentable. Certain teachings are deemed "no longer relevant," "not cross-culture capable," or "metaphorical" leaving the holy book with fewer and fewer passages that are viewed as authoritative. This is a form of slow death for faith.

Each round of reinterpreting is one more step down a staircase to cast aside what was an item of required belief but is now deemed theological rubbish. What lies down the steps is a basement with nothing in it.

If an all-powerful, personal, loving God had clearly and accurately self-revealed, neither of these two responses—religious fundamentalism or the constant pruning of sacred teachings—would be required.

Coming up with a workable plan for self-revelation wouldn't be that difficult for a God with no limits on wisdom, power, or communication skills.

Such a God could choose to be seen or heard by everyone in the world at the same time. He could attenuate the light of his radiance to avoid blinding those who see. He could turn down the volume of his voice to prevent it from overpowering mortals who hear it. Such a God could translate, clarify, and illuminate so that every human could hear and understand.

Or, God could create and send divine messengers to different parts of the world—all at the same time. He could empower each emissary to perform validating acts so far beyond human means that no one would doubt they were his messengers. And all these spokespersons would surely share the same clear message about who God is and what God requires of someone who wants to respond to him in a positive way.

And it would make sense to arrange for periodic repetitions of whatever method was chosen for self-revelation since, with the passing of time, new generations would be likely to doubt old stories about earlier revelations.

There are multiple ways an all-powerful, all-knowing, loving God could self-reveal in a manner that would end all doubt, but no such self-revelations have occurred. And therein lies the basis for my second question:

How could a loving God who created a universe do such a poor job at clearly revealing who he is and what he expects?

3 – The Germ Warfare Question

You could argue that the earliest humans didn't need to know the earth is round instead of flat. They had more important concerns. One could contend it wasn't important for primitive people to understand that the earth revolves and orbits the sun—no reason to rush that discovery along. And was there actually a need for early humans to know the earth is billions of years old?

But it's hard to argue that any time was too soon for humans to learn about the microscopic organisms that cause so much sickness and death—germs.

The Cognitive Revolution began 70,000 years ago when our ancestors started to develop new ways of thinking and communicating that included—for the first time—an ability to transmit information about things that don't exist.[9] Let's use the beginning of the Cognitive Revolution as a starting point for a period in which the world has been populated by people much like you and me—people who could make up stories.

If the last 70,000 years were a 24-hour day that just ended at midnight, the time at which the world began to move forward with an understanding of germs that generated revolutionary new ways to prevent sickness and death was 11:57 PM.

That's 69,866 years of pervasive germ ignorance.

As late as the mid-1800s doctors were still delivering babies after coming directly from autopsies without washing their hands.[10] Before the 20th century, excrement was piled high in cities, and their rivers were thick and sticky with waste. Drinking water was likely to be drawn from the same brown water used for washing clothes.[11]

We have no historical records of the human suffering and premature deaths caused by germs during most of this 69,866-year span, but we know that the average life expectancy of a hunter-gatherer—the way of life for most of this period—is 33 years.[12] This doesn't mean that no one lived past their thirties. Keep in mind that if you calculate the average lifespan of two individuals—one who died at 60 and another who died immediately after birth—the average will be 30 years.

While we might learn a few things from the eating habits of hunter-gatherers, it was a life where a simple accident—a flesh wound or a compound fracture—could be a death sentence. Childbirth was a roll of the dice for mother and infant. An abscessed tooth could spell your doom, and a thirst-quenching drink of water could be deadly.

The agricultural revolution began about 12,000 years ago when humans began to settle and grow crops. It was ultimately a move toward towns and cities, and as more humans began to live in confined spaces alongside domesticated animals, the potential for the spread of lethal communicable diseases increased dramatically.[13]

The first cases of flu date back 6,000 years. An ancient medical text described the symptoms of malaria in 2700 BC. Smallpox is at least 3,000 years old. The death toll for this triad of contagious diseases and others like them is in the hundreds of millions.[14]

Typhoid—a highly contagious disease caused by the bacteria Salmonella typhi and spread through contaminated water and food supplies—wiped out one-third of the population of Athens between 430 and 424 BC.[15]

Cases of the bubonic plague, caused by the bacteria Yersinia pestis, were reported as early as the sixth century A.D. when it took the lives of more than 25 million people over two centuries. An outbreak started in 1348 and killed 25 to 50 percent of the population of Europe in a three-year period—in some areas, there were not enough survivors to bury the dead.[16]

Tuberculosis—an organism whose existence predates the

first human settlements—is caused by the bacteria Mycobacterium tuberculosis. The disease killed an estimated one-fourth of the adult population of Europe in the 19th century.[17]

Between 1831 and 1854, tens of thousands of people in England died of cholera. The current theory was that the disease was caused by "miasmata in the atmosphere." When an outbreak occurred in London's Soho district, Dr. John Snow, a pioneer in epidemiology, had another theory—that the disease was spread by contaminated water.

The Soho epidemic began on August 31, 1854, and soon became what Snow later described as "the most terrible outbreak of cholera which ever occurred in the kingdom." In three days, 127 people living in or around Broad Street died. Days later, most of the residents had fled their homes and shuttered their shops. By the end of September, 616 residents of Soho had died.

Dr. Snow, interviewing the family members of victims, identified the source of the outbreak as a public water pump on Broad Street. He persuaded authorities to disable the pump, and when they did so, the spread of cholera stopped.

A local minister had other ideas. Reverend Henry Whitehead, believing the outbreak was caused by divine intervention, had undertaken his own investigation. But he ended up recognizing that Snow was correct, and helped

Snow find the source of the contamination—water used to wash the diaper of a baby infected with cholera had found its way into a leaking cesspool located three feet from the Broad Street well.

From a modern vantage point, it's obvious that Snow was on target, but the local Board of Health rejected his findings, and one year later no changes had been made in response to the evidence he presented.[18]

But the light bulb of discovery was burning in other places. In 1861 Louis Pasteur, a French chemist, published his germ theory asserting that microscopic organisms cause disease.[19]

Between 1865 and 1869, deaths resulting from surgery in the Male Accident Ward in Scotland's Glasgow Royal Infirmary dropped from 45% to 15%. The reason: Surgeon Joseph Lister—pursuing his own version of a germ theory—had introduced the practice of sterilizing surgeons' hands and operating instruments. Gradually, the international medical community began to accept Lister's evidence that surgery should be carried out under antiseptic conditions.[20]

Building upon Pasteur's work, German physician Robert Koch announced in 1876 that he had proved that the bacterium Bacillus anthracis causes anthrax.[21] Pasteur confirmed Koch's discovery and in 1881 successfully vaccinated sheep outside of Paris to protect them from anthrax.[22]

Like a steam locomotive inching out of the station, the battle against disease-causing microbes was on its way. By the turn of the century, vaccines had been developed for rabies [23] and cholera (1885), [24] typhoid (1896), [25] and bubonic plague (1897).[26]

As the 20th century got underway, the train was barreling down the tracks. In 1908, Jersey City, New Jersey, became the first city in the U.S. to practice disinfection of community drinking water [27] paving the way for water chlorination as the norm for any modern town or city.

Vaccines for tuberculosis, diphtheria, scarlet fever, yellow fever, typhus, encephalitis, and polio were developed between 1921 and 1952.[28]

The discovery of penicillin in 1928 marked the beginning of the antibiotic age. Before penicillin, there was no useful treatment for infections like pneumonia and rheumatic fever. Hospitals were filled with patients suffering from blood poisoning as the result of a cut or scratch—and there was little doctors could do.[29]

Antibiotics, vaccinations, handwashing, public sewage systems, chlorinated drinking water, and increased public awareness of the importance of cleanliness prolonged the lives of billions. [30] The evidence is in worldwide life expectancy figures that—like the progress that created the numbers—were first noteworthy, then remarkable.

For most of human history, the average lifespan has

hovered one or two years above or below the age of 31.[31] Between 1770 and 1900, the worldwide average for life expectancy increased from 29 to 33 years. Then, between 1900 and 2015, **worldwide life expectancy rose from 33 to 71 years.**[32]

Medical science has given humans a new lease on life, but how sad that the leap in lifespan occurred minutes before midnight on the 70,000-year clock.

Jesus has been hailed as the Great Physician, but the human lifespan revolution took hold in the 20th century, not the first century. These incredibly improved life expectancy statistics require that Jesus take a back seat to lifesavers like John Snow, Louis Pasteur, Robert Koch, Joseph Lister, Jonas Salk, and many more. And this fact is the springboard for my third question:

Why didn't Jesus say anything about germs?

Not only did Jesus fail to mention germs, but he steered his listeners in the wrong direction when he told them not to worry about washing their hands.

> The Pharisees and some of the teachers of the law who had come from Jerusalem gathered around Jesus and saw some of his disciples eating food with hands that were defiled, that is, unwashed. (The Pharisees and all the Jews do not eat unless they give their hands a

ceremonial washing, holding to the tradition of the elders. When they come from the marketplace they do not eat unless they wash. And they observe many other traditions, such as the washing of cups, pitchers and kettles.) So the Pharisees and teachers of the law asked Jesus, "Why don't your disciples live according to the tradition of the elders instead of eating their food with defiled hands?" [33]

Jesus gave a lengthy reply about hypocrisy, then said:

Nothing outside a person can defile them by going into them. Rather, it is what comes out of a person that defiles them.[34]

In his comments, Jesus was focused on the importance of inner spiritual change over outward religious ceremony. But wouldn't this have been a great time to explain that they should wash their hands for health purposes, a good time to tell people about germs, a good time to talk about why they should be careful where they get their drinking water, along with a few tips about sewage disposal?

Wouldn't such a simple act of education have saved countless lives—exponentially more than all the people Jesus miraculously healed during his ministry?

And what a powerful proof it would have been that Jesus really was who he claimed to be if he had chosen to impart some basic knowledge about germs and sanitation—

information that could have dramatically altered human lifespans wherever his teachings were followed.

Instead, his message was pretty much: "You don't need to wash your hands, but if someone's sick, it could be a demon." And 1800 years later, people in Christian England still didn't understand that drinking water needed to be isolated from sewage. The first inclination of a local minister was that a cholera outbreak was punishment from God. This ignorance about germs led to death—over and over throughout history—until science discovered the microscopic organisms that can make people sick.

Why didn't the God of the universe—walking among humankind in the flesh as Jesus—do a sidebar talk on germs?

As a Christian minister, I would have answered the question something like this:

> I don't have an easy answer to the problem of why Jesus didn't provide some simple but practical information about germs and sanitation.
>
> I do know that Jesus emptied himself of his unlimited knowledge before taking the form of a man so that he could fully experience humanity. And I know that suffering and death in this world is part of the curse delivered in the Garden of Eden. I know that Jesus taught

us to do all we can to help those who are sick and suffering. And I know that when we get to heaven, we can ask God to help us understand the things like this that make no sense to us in this life.

We can also appreciate that Christianity—over time—helped engender the idea that we live in an orderly, cause-and-effect world, a world where the logic of scientific inquiry makes sense. We can be grateful that God created and gifted medical scientists with the intelligent minds, probing curiosity, and unrelenting perseverance that led to the great medical discoveries of our era.

And we can always take comfort in the promise that in heaven there will be no sickness, disease, or death.

But I finally reached a point where even my own answers no longer made sense to me, and I found myself asking: Why did God watch quietly while it took humans multiple millenniums—until three minutes before midnight on the 70,000-year clock—to discover and react to the danger posed by germs?

Imagine finding yourself in a position similar to God's fatherhood of humanity. You are living in a remote, isolated area, and have been put in charge of 300 children between the ages of 10 and 15. None of these young people know anything about how to survive. There are no other adults around. You are—for all practical purposes—the parent of the 300 children.

Faced with this important task, you opt for an odd strategy: You decide to stay out of sight and remain silent. Despite your having all the resources and knowledge these children need to survive and thrive, you decide it will be interesting to see how they handle things on their own.

Naturally, the results are disastrous. Without the benefit of your parental insights, you watch as—one-by-one—many of your children die: from drinking contaminated water or failing to wash their hands at the appropriate time, from eating poisonous foods, or by succumbing to common illnesses.

The children who manage to survive the early rounds of losses sometimes learn from the deaths of the others, but sometimes they repeat the same mistakes. And they make up foolish—sometimes harmful—ways to treat the maladies they commonly face.

You watch in silence. You could help. You could explain. You have all the information they need, but you just watch.

It would make no sense to argue that your actions were driven by any version of parental love if you acted this way. In fact, we have a name for this parenting style. It's called child abuse.

Decent parents protect their kids from danger. If your toddler grabs the liquid Drano container, you don't watch in silence.

But that is exactly what God the Heavenly Father had done through the ages. He just watches, invisible and silent.

Why?

God had been watching silently for thousands of years by the time Jesus came along. It was late in the game, but couldn't the Son of God—the one described as the Great Physician—have made a greater contribution to human health than healing a few people while he was on earth?

Why didn't Jesus say anything about germs?

4 – The Better Plan Question

Early Christians battled for centuries over which books should be included in the New Testament. Some groups believed the Old Testament was inspired while others didn't. There were segments of Christianity that believed Jesus was divine as well as human while other Christian groups believed he was divine, but not human. Still others saw him as a man who was adopted as the son of God.[35]

The list of theological controversies was long in the second and third centuries, but eventually, winners emerged, and the victories in these battles shaped what we now regard orthodox or non-heretical Christianity.[36]

Christians are still arguing about many aspects of their theology, but there are some key concepts upon which most Christians agree. One example is the belief that Jesus is fully God and fully man. Another area of general agreement is the storyline for humanity's fall and God's plan of redemption. What follows is a summary of its key points.

God created humans with the capacity to be in a meaningful, loving relationship with him. To be meaningful-relationship-capable, humans had to be equipped with free will to allow them to accept or reject God's love.

As the all-powerful creator of everything, God could have given humans a behavioral autopilot that could not be overridden—providing a constant state of obedience and ensuring that every individual lived in an uninterrupted, meaningful relationship with God. But how could a relationship with God be meaningful, loving, and authentic if humans were relational robots who had no choice but to obey? Free will was essential.

The importance of exercising free will came into play shortly after creation when Adam and Eve—living in the Garden of Eden in a state of innocent fellowship with God—made a decision with life-altering results for all of humanity.

God gave one commandment: "You are free to eat from any tree in the garden; but you must not eat from the tree of the knowledge of good and evil, for when you eat from it you will certainly die."[37]

No other tree was off-limits, just the fruit of the tree of the knowledge of good and evil. The creator of these first two humans—never having been a parent before—didn't realize that once he told them not to eat the fruit from one tree, that one tree became the most enticing spot in the garden.

It didn't help matters that a talking snake—described as craftier than any of the wild animals—encouraged Eve to take the first bite. Adam joined Eve in the God-human-relationship-altering act of eating the forbidden fruit.

When God came walking in the garden, Adam and Even hid. They were ashamed and frightened—the penalty for what they had done was clear: death. God found them and gave them an opportunity to fess up. Then the cursing started.

Snakes were cursed to crawl on their bellies and eat dust. Childbirth would become severely painful for women, and husbands would rule over their wives. [38] Men would engage in painful toil—combating thorns and thistles—to harvest food from the ground.

Adam and Eve were evicted from their garden paradise, forbidden to eat from the tree of life, and scratched off the immortality roster. They would die and return to the dust of the earth.

That day, sin, judgment, and death became part of the human experience. And somehow, all humans were affected by the disobedience of the first man and woman as clearly stated in Romans 5:2: "…just as sin entered the world through one man, and death through sin, and in this way death came to all people, because all sinned."

Some Christians believe that all humans inherit not only a sinful nature from Adam and Eve but also their guilt. Thus, in their view, babies need to be quickly baptized to cover the guilt of this original sin.

Other Christians hold that we inherit an inclination toward sin that is so powerful that it leads every one of us to incur our own guilt by engaging in sin once we are old enough to know right from wrong.

Either way, we're all sinners and we all have a problem.

God is holy, and that means he cannot abide in the presence of sin. God wants a meaningful, loving relationship with everyone, but options for a close-up, positive God connection are off the table when sin is present. So, humans cannot experience the loving relationship God wants with them until they experience the cleansing of forgiveness.

Although the Genesis account of the fall of man offers no hint of a plan for redemption or a second chance at life that never ends, if we fast forward to the New Testament, we can see the ultimate redemption plan unfolding.

It's a plan that embraces eternity. Humans who find forgiveness will live with God in heaven forever, but the unforgiven will be consigned to never-ending punishment in hell.[39]

How is forgiveness possible? Forgiveness requires a

sacrifice for sin, and a lamb without blemish sacrificed at
the Jewish Temple in Jerusalem was not enough. The
sacrifice of a sinless man was needed.

Enter Jesus, Stage Left. Jesus—the Son of God who
became a man—is the only person who ever lived a sinless
life. Only Jesus is qualified to be the sacrifice for our sins,
and that's the reason he died on the cross. God used a
Roman execution to carry out his plan: "Behold, the Lamb
of God, who takes away the sin of the world!"[40]

And this is what I preached:

> Jesus died for your sins. But you must accept
> his sacrifice. You must confess your
> sinfulness and trust him to forgive you. You
> must believe in him. You must receive him as
> your savior. You must commit your life to
> follow him as your king.

This plan of salvation is easier to digest when you hear it
for the first time as a child—a time before critical thinking
when you are compliant and always believe what your
parents and teachers tell you. You just accept each part of
the story as it is spoon-fed to you, and it seems like a
logical plan. By the time you're old enough to think
critically, the "plan" is so ingrained in your thinking that
it's extremely difficult to step back and look at it
objectively.

Conversions of adults with no prior Christian experience

are rare unless part of some wave of cultural or generational change in a region. But when they do occur, it is likely to be in times of personal crisis when many of the usual coping mechanisms aren't working like they usually do and there is a dramatic level of openness to trying something new.

In such instances—when an individual is ready to try anything so as not to feel helpless and defeated—the plan of salvation may be swallowed like a magic pill. Even as a new adult believer, you are just one individual responding to centuries of dogma and seeking acceptance from a congregation of believers who regard the gospel plan of redemption as above any questioning.

Put all this together—facing a crisis, coping mechanisms diminished, wanting acceptance by a group—and you are likely to accept the plan with fewer questions than you would ask when buying a car. You want the gospel story to be true. You want it to work because if it works, you've made the right decision, and you can believe that your life is going to get better.

It took me decades, but when I finally stepped back far enough to get a high-altitude view, I had many questions. The questions weren't necessarily new, but I felt a fresh freedom to purse any query—old or new—and I did just that.

Here are some of the issues that entreated me for a better explanation than my long-held answers.

Silly Story

God's salvation plan for all humanity starts with what by any rational way of thinking is an awfully silly story. Prior to the account of the fall in the garden in the third chapter of Genesis, the first chapter asserts that our 4.5 billion-year-old earth and everything on it was created in only a few days. The first man was handmade by God, then—in what looks remarkably like an afterthought—the first woman was created from the man's rib. (Did God add reproductive organs to Adam after deciding to create Eve?) And we learn nothing about the Neanderthals.

The story of the fall of man features a talking snake as the tempter—a leading role that resulted in the curse of not being able to walk. It's a story with magic trees and folk explanations for pain in childbirth, how humans started wearing clothes, and why men must work for food. It's a story with an omnipresent, transcendent God walking in a garden looking for the only two humans on earth.

It's a story in which the eternal destiny of all humans hangs in the balance as the first man and woman—standing naked in a garden—decide to do the one thing God told them not to do.

The only way many contemporary Christians can handle the Genesis account of the fall is by viewing it as a mythical story that still conveys the essential theological truth that humans are sinful and need redemption. But viewing Adam and Eve as symbolic is something the rest of the Bible doesn't do. The Apostle Paul saw Adam as one individual in the same way Jesus was one person.

> For if the many died by the trespass of the one
> man, how much more did God's grace and the
> gift that came by the grace of the one man,
> Jesus Christ, overflow to the many![41]

Two humans made from scratch ruin everything for the
rest of us, and we didn't even get to vote them in as our
representatives!

Loud Silence

From the standpoint of the redemption narrative, the
rebellion of Adam and Eve infected all who would follow
them with a spiritual virus called sin, and it created a life-
or-death need for a perfect human who would be worthy
as a sacrifice for the sins of all.

A little patience was in order since it was thousands of
years later when Jesus was born in Bethlehem. The
Gospels of Matthew and Luke tell us about his birth and
infancy. And Luke's Gospel tells the story of Jesus's visit
to the Temple in Jerusalem at age 12—where he spent
several days in discussion with religious teachers, amazing
everyone with his understanding of the things of God.
Luke ends his account of Jesus's temple visit with these
words: "And Jesus grew in wisdom and stature, and in
favor with God and man."[42]

That's the last report on anything Jesus did or said until he
begins his ministry around the age of 30. The temple visit

at age 12 marks the start of 18 years of silence about the life of the only person who—according to Christianity—ever managed to avoid committing even one sinful thought or act.[43]

Why do we know absolutely nothing about the world's only perfect life between the ages of 13 and 29?

For decades I wasn't troubled by this information gap. "God has his reasons" is a good multi-purpose tool for handling hard questions related to faith. But today, I see the Bible's silence on these years of Jesus's life as a glaring and troubling omission.

We have one sinless human being in all of history and the only records we have between infancy and age 30 are a few lines about a trip to Jerusalem and the terse statement that he "grew in wisdom and stature, and in favor with God and man"?

I could not count the times when as a preacher, I declared that, "Jesus showed us how to live." I would point to his sayings, parables, and acts of love. But all the references I could make to the actions of Jesus were in the context of a man who had left family, vocation, and any normal sense of daily life to walk from town to town with a band of disciples in training.

If only we had more stories of Jesus's early years that clearly portrayed real-life examples of what doing the right thing looks like—in as many situations as possible. How wonderful it would have been to have a treasure trove of perfect examples for how life should be lived from the more "normal" times in Jesus's life.

Think of how helpful it would be if teenage Christians could read true stories of all that Jesus did when he was an adolescent. Regardless of centuries of cultural changes since he walked on the earth, surely such stories would have provided a gold mine of examples to follow.

And what if we had the details of Jesus's life in his twenties? How did he transition from adolescence to adulthood? How did he build strong, meaningful friendships? How did he deal with sexual temptation? How did he practice integrity in his work— presumably as a carpenter? A story of his gladly redoing a project for an unhappy customer would have been a good model.

Isn't it true that we often fail to make the right choice and do the right thing when we aren't quite sure what is right? And isn't it true that we're more likely to know what is the right thing to do when we have an example to follow?

If you're a person of faith, and it's hard to connect with my disappointment that we have no information about what Jesus said or did for 18 years of his life, humor me briefly. Imagine you've never heard about Jesus, and someone tells you a story about the only perfectly sinless human to ever walk the earth. Then at some point, this individual casually remarks that the only information about this person's life beyond childhood covers a period one to three years at the end of his life.[44]

Wouldn't you immediately question why there wasn't more evidence to validate that this individual did in fact live a life in which no faults could be found?

Wouldn't you wonder why the God empowering this perfect life failed to ensure that someone wrote about events from its every year?

And wouldn't you wonder if the real reason for this loud silence was that the details of this life at an earlier stage needed to be concealed to sell the story of a perfect life?

Bargain Sacrifice

The reason that sinners need a sacrifice for their sins is that God cannot reside in the presence of sin. We can't be connected to God in a meaningful way—including going to heaven—unless we are cleansed of sin, and we can't be cleansed unless we are forgiven, and we can't be forgiven without a perfect sacrifice for our sins. That's why Jesus had to make his way to the cross. At the core of Christian theology is the concept that Jesus's death on the cross was unlike any other crucifixion because he bore the sins of everyone in the world in those six hours.

For decades—as a minister and a faithful Christian—I never questioned any of this. But when I began to critically review the salvation plan I had believed and shared with others for so long, I started thinking about the size of the debt Jesus paid on the cross.

I wanted to figure out how many people deserved eternity in hell and multiply that number by some finite representation of the years each person might spend in hell if they had to pay their own debt to God. After a little research, I began with the assumption that—including the 7 billion-plus people alive today—a total of around 108 billion people have lived on the earth. Recognizing that according to the gospel message, every one of these 108 billion people deserves an eternity in hell, I had the first number needed for my theological calculations.

Having no way to multiply by eternity, I arbitrarily used a 10-billion-year sentence in hell for each of the 108 billion individuals. The result was a total of 1,080,000,000,000,000,000,000 years of required punishment time in hell—if we all got what we deserve. That's my finite calculation of the debt that had to be paid by Jesus on the cross.

Christians believe that Jesus took the place of all humanity when he suffered for six hours on the cross. Six hours on the cross canceled out a debt of 1,080,000,000,000,000,000,000 years of deserved torture time.[45]

I used to say that's why Jesus cried out "My God, My God, why have you forsaken me"[46] before he died. Billions of years of punishment were condensed into six hours on the cross during which Jesus felt the full weight of the sins of all people.

Don't get me wrong. Death by Roman crucifixion was a torturous, horrible way for any person to die. And the idea of anyone carrying the pain, shame, and guilt of the sins of all people for even an instant is unimaginable. But it's hard not to think that however great the substitutionary pain on the cross may have been, six hours is not a lot of time to cancel out 1,080,000,000,000,000,000,000,000 plus years of fiery punishment. I don't know about you, but that's what I call a bargain.

And then you have the issue of "dying" for the sins of all people. Jesus was dead for three days before his resurrection. So, wouldn't it be more accurate to say that what he gave was six hours of incredible pain plus three days in the realm of death?

Pause Rewind

Now that our review of God's plan of redemption has covered the original sin of Adam and Eve, the perfect life of Jesus, and his atoning sacrifice, let's pause and rewind to the Garden of Eden story.

Regardless of the Old and New Testament's view that Adam and Eve were the first two humans, it makes sense that modern, science-sensitive Christians would choose to see these two as characters in a mythical story. But here we have a wonderful example of a solution that creates a much bigger problem, a problem clearly and powerfully articulated in a Tweet by Oxford author M.G. Harris.

If evolution is true, then Adam and Eve didn't

exist. And our "fallen nature" is our evolved behavior, created by the need to survive. So, what did Jesus die for? Why are all humans so guilty at birth that they need a blood sacrifice of the most perfect being in existence to atone for something that was coded into our being through no fault of our own?[47]

While the weight of that conundrum is soaking in, let's fast forward back to our previous stopping point and resume our walkthrough of God's plan of redemption.

Resurrection Problems

As a Christian, my belief in the resurrection of Jesus was the ultimate firewall against destructive doubt. His resurrection was the event that set him apart from all other religious leaders. It was proof of his victory over death, and reason to believe Christians like me would live forever. And it had to be true: There were witnesses. In one case 500 people saw the resurrected Jesus.

But as my skeptical review of faith moved along, the old hypnotic trance was fading. I no longer felt compelled to ignore hard questions about the things I had believed for so long—and this included questions about the resurrection of Jesus. I found myself asking questions like:

- Why do the Gospels' accounts of finding the empty tomb vary in so many of the details?

- Why is it that Mark mentions no resurrection

appearances? Why are the resurrection accounts in Matthew, Luke, and John so different?

- Why were the post-resurrection appearances of Jesus limited to only a few people—and only to those who were already believers?

- Why did some disciples who saw the resurrected Jesus doubt?

- Why was the resurrected Jesus hard to recognize at certain times, but not at other times?

- Why did the resurrected Jesus come and go with such unpredictability?

- Why, after his resurrection, did Jesus both welcome and prohibit being touched?

- If Jesus appeared to 500 people, why do we not have one specific name from this group of witnesses?

- Why were no written accounts provided by the actual witnesses to the resurrection—immediately after it happened?

- Why, in the years before the New Testament books were written, did God choose to rely on decades of word-of-mouth accounts that surely morphed, expanded, left out details, and added this and that to embellish the story?

- Why did God wait 35 years to inspire the author of Mark's Gospel to write down the story of Jesus's life—making Mark the earliest of the four Gospels—and why then did his account leave out the resurrection of

Jesus?[48]

Not only are the preceding questions troubling, but if the gospel story of Jesus is what it proclaims itself to be—a message for every continent, every generation, every single human being—we could surely expect the evidence for the resurrection of Jesus to be irrefutable in multiple ways:

- We could expect that the resurrected Jesus would want to be seen by as many people as possible.

- We could imagine him announcing: For the next two weeks I will receive all visitors at 19 Temple Lane in Jerusalem.

- We could expect that Jesus would appear to non-believers as well as believers.

- We could anticipate more consistency in the reports of sightings of the resurrected Jesus.

- We could assume that he would appear to large numbers of people—repeatedly—and that someone would take names.

- We could count on Jesus appearing in more than one limited geographical region.

And since irrefutable evidence is something we have a right to expect for this once-in-history event, it's fair to ask, "Why didn't the resurrected Jesus appear to the Roman Emperor Tiberius Caesar?"

Imagine that after rising from the tomb, Jesus miraculously

transports Governor Pilate and all the Roman soldiers who were present at his crucifixion right into the room where Tiberius is sitting. To get their attention, Jesus immediately levitates all the occupants of the room to one foot above the floor. Next, one-by-one, Pilate and each of the Roman soldiers who saw Jesus die testify that the man standing beside them—Jesus, the man who just made them all appear in the room—is the prophet they executed and buried a few days earlier.

Such an event would surely have accelerated the Roman Empire's embrace of Christianity by almost 300 years—spurring dramatic growth for Christianity and preventing the reported deaths of Christian martyrs who died under multiple persecutions prior to the Roman Empire's decriminalization of Christianity in 313 A.D. And such an event—recorded in secular history—would have provided us with more convincing historical evidence that Jesus did rise from death.[49]

Better still, the resurrected Jesus could have gone on a Worldwide Resurrection Tour with stops in China and every city, town, and village in the world.

But let's assume that despite all the deficiencies in the resurrection story, the Gospel accounts are accurate in reporting that multiple followers of Jesus testified that they saw the resurrected Jesus at different times during the 40 days after his death and that at least some of these disciples were willing to die rather than recant that belief. Doesn't this prove Jesus rose from the dead?

The fact that one or more individuals believed they saw Jesus alive after his death means just that—some individuals were convinced they saw Jesus after he died. But it does not prove Jesus was alive after his death.

All through history, adherents of various faiths, have claimed to witness miracles and supernatural appearances. If such events are in line with one's own faith, they are believed. Otherwise, they are discarded.

In modern times, many Roman Catholics have claimed to see the Virgin Mary—sometimes even as a group. The same Christians who rely on centuries-old accounts of the post-resurrection appearances of Jesus as irrefutable evidence of the truth of his victory over death dismiss contemporary claims of appearances of the Virgin Mary. And they do so without a moment of contemplation—the reason being that they don't believe that the Virgin Mary is making live appearances regardless of who testifies otherwise. It's the same kind of evidence, but it's categorically denied by those who don't want to believe what the evidence is supposed to prove.

And if believing something so strongly that you are willing to die for that belief means that what you believe must be true, then what about September 11, 2001? Should we then adopt the beliefs of the terrorists who died for what they believed?[50]

One more thing. The growth of Christianity exploded after it was made legal, then became the official religion of the

Roman Empire. But up until 300 A.D., the average annual growth rate was less than 4%. That's a rate that—like compound interest—produces dramatic results over a long period of time. But it's not an expansion rate with which any modern church-growth-oriented pastor would be happy.

This slow growth rate seems inconsistent with Christianity's belief that its founder was executed, stayed dead for three days, then came back to life. It's a poor fit for a religion that claims to be supernaturally powered, pledges to turn believers into new people, and promises victory over death. It seems out of sync with a powerhouse kind of faith whose truth is instantly compelling.

Some Christian writers attribute the initially slow growth rate to the fact that Christians were subject to intermittent persecutions during the new faith's first centuries. But the idea that the explosive growth of a resurrection-empowered faith could begin only after it was sanctioned by the world's most powerful empire seems counter-intuitive. Slow growth—even in the face of persecution—seems to be out of character for a movement that is the heart of a creator God's own plan to make himself known to all people.

Excessive Casualties

But let's say that none of the issues raised in the preceding paragraphs really matter. Let's say the Genesis story isn't silly and passes muster. Let's say we accept that God is holy and cannot reside in the presence of sin. Let's accept the proposition that Jesus was the son of God who came to earth as a man, lived a perfect life, died on the cross for our sins, and rose from the dead.

A pressing problem still requires our attention: Something went terribly wrong with God's plan of redemption. A loving God created meaningful-relationship-capable humans to experience his love, but a safe estimate is that three out of four of the 108 billion individuals who have lived thus far will end up suffering for eternity in hell.

My three-out-of-four-in-hell estimate is based on the fact that about 2.2 billion of the 7.5 billion people alive today are Christians, and Jesus was clear that not everyone who claims to be a Christian really is. So, hell must be one gigantic piece of real estate!

How could a place of eternal torment populated by 80 billion or so of the 108 billion people who have lived on the earth be part of any plan conceived by a loving God? And how could an all-knowing God not realize ahead of time that this result was inevitable?

The issue is further complicated by the fact that billions never have a fair opportunity to hear, believe, and live the Christian life because of where or when they were born.

I grew up in West Texas where you couldn't drive for more than a few minutes without seeing a Baptist Church. What if I had been born in North Korea or Somalia? Would my chances of becoming a Christian have been just as good as they were in Texas? Absolutely not![51]

Eventually, I had to ask regarding God's redemption plan: Couldn't God have made us so we weren't doomed to disobey?

The standard Christian answer is no. Since God made humans to have a meaningful relationship with him, he had to give us free will, and that made disobedience inevitable.

The only other option would have been for God to create obedient robots, but such humans would not have been meaningful-relationship-capable. How could God delight in our obedience if we could do nothing else?

It's an accepted fact that as far as Christians are concerned, God could not make us so we would always be obedient and have our obedience mean anything.

But there's one big problem with describing a meaningful-relationship-capable and obedient-only existence as something God could not make happen: *It is exactly what the Bible teaches God will do in heaven.*

In heaven, believers will always obey while still having a meaningful relationship with God that is pleasing to him and to the believer.

Heaven will be filled with people who no longer sin, and there's not the slightest implication they will be robots.

Somehow, in heaven, all inhabitants will be meaningful-relationship-capable and free-willed but completely obedient. **Apparently, what God could not do here on earth, he will easily do in heaven.**

So why didn't God skip the Garden of Eden and all that followed? No need for a worldwide flood to kill all the sinners. No Tower of Babel to knock down. No Sodom and Gomorrah to destroy. No cycle of disobedience and recovery for God's people. No need for Jesus to suffer and die. And no need to build a place called hell known for its extreme heat and massive size.

This alternate plan would be simple: *Create everyone in the same state described under the current redemption plan for the inhabitants of heaven.* Make everyone meaningful-relationship-capable, put them in obedient-only mode, and let them live happily ever after. Skip the pain of living in a fallen world, the sinful failures, and the uncertainty about one's eternal destiny.

No "Get Out of Jail Free' card would be needed because there would be no jail. Everyone would simply go straight to heaven.

Why not?

A common Christian response would sound something like the following:

> God gave us free will so we could freely

choose him and enjoy the results of a freely given, freely received relationship.

We shouldn't presume to know how God could have created us or what alternate plans he could have fashioned for us to be in relationship with him.

God doesn't send anyone to hell. People go to hell when they choose to reject God's offer of forgiveness and life.

As for people in remote places where they may not hear the gospel, we can only say that God is fair, and it would make sense if he gave such individuals some chance—some way—to accept him that is not currently within our grasp of understanding and does not mitigate the truth of the gospel message.

Another standard Christian response is:

Sending everyone straight to heaven would make things too easy. Faith must be tested. We need to prove ourselves to God.

But is that how a father or mother loves their children? Must boys and girls prove their love to Mom and Dad or otherwise be cast into a furnace?

Don't good parents love their children unconditionally—

providing the best for them just because they love them?

Don't most human parents know their children will disobey at times, know that consequences should be proportional, and never want their children to die because of some bad decision they make—no matter how regretful the decision might be?

What parent would place a child in an impossibly difficult situation then torture the child for a lifetime when they failed?

God's plan for salvation as described in the Bible and interpreted by most Christians just doesn't add up. When you really think about this whole scheme, it sounds like divine nonsense. Even a human parent could do better. And this is the basis for the last of my four questions:

Why would a heavenly father condemn most of his children to eternal torment when he could send them all straight to heaven?

5 – The One Simple Answer

T he New Testament exhorts Christians to always be ready to give an answer for why they believe in the gospel message.[52] And that was one of my goals— to always be prepared to give a compelling response to any challenge to my Christian faith.

As an evangelical minister, I had answers for each of the questions raised in the preceding chapters

If you asked me, **"Why does faith in the resurrected, empowered Jesus generate such inconsistent results?"** I would have stressed that all Christians need to be sure their initial commitment to Jesus meets all the necessary requirements because you can't expect a faith that's not genuine to produce consistent results.

And I would assert that life-changing conversions do happen, that every week I could see genuine spiritual power at work in the lives of committed believers who worked to make sure they were in constant fellowship with God.

I would affirm that being a Christian—regardless of how committed you might be—doesn't make you sinless. The Christian faith is a journey toward a kind of spiritual perfection that will be finished only when we reach heaven.

And I might have shared a line I learned in seminary: Faith that fizzles before it finishes had a fatal flaw from the first.

When confronted with the second question, **"How could a loving God who created a universe do such a poor job at clearly revealing who he is and what he expects?"** I would have asserted that we do have a clear and unmistakably true revelation from God, that God has clearly revealed himself to humanity in Jesus, and that the Bible is the infallible, trustworthy, and complete record of God's revelation.

If you asked minister me, **"Why didn't Jesus say anything about germs?"** I would have noted that Jesus emptied himself of his limitless knowledge so that he could fully experience humanity. I would remind that sickness, suffering, and death exist in the world because of the fall of humanity in the Garden of Eden. I would affirm that there will be no disease or death in heaven. But I would also admit that I didn't have an easy answer for the scope of human suffering in the world.

Finally, if you asked, **"Why would a heavenly father condemn most of his children to eternal torment when he could send them all straight to heaven?"** I would have answered that we shouldn't presume to know how God could have created us and what plan he could have fashioned for us to live in a meaningful relationship with him. And I would have added that God doesn't send anyone to hell. People go to hell when they use their free will to choose rejection of God's offer of forgiveness and life.

In my years as a minister, there were many other questions about faith, but I had what I considered a reasonable answer for just about any question I might be asked. And when I didn't have a good answer, there was always the multi-purpose, catch-all response: "That's something we'll have to ask God when we get to heaven."

But none of my old, carefully worded defenses of faith make sense anymore.

What happened?

After living and leading in the church for decades, I saw no consistent evidence of an ongoing supernatural presence—and I wanted to see that evidence with all that was in me. The apparent absence of a supernatural presence was at the top of a long list of *exceptions to the rule of faith*—a list I had been building since my early years in ministry, a list that with time became more and more impossible to ignore.

A series of life events pushed me out of my comfortable nest in the life of the church, and with that expulsion I found a new freedom to think without limits about faith and all the exceptions to its rules.

I didn't change overnight.

The disintegration of my Christian beliefs took place over a period of years and often felt more like something that was happening to me than something I was doing.

Frequently I was startled when I heard myself expressing some new belief that I could not remember consciously thinking about. It would usually occur when I was involved in a conversation about religion. I would express my view on the issue being discussed, and later I would think, "Did I say that? Yes, I did. Is that what I believe? Yes, that's what I believe now."

I was the one ruminating and contemplating, but as I changed one belief, related topics would reshuffle, and sometimes I was surprised when I heard myself making a statement that represented the results of this quickly evolving process. My brain was realigning what I viewed as true and what I viewed as false, occasionally informing me of its progress by letting me hear myself say something that reflected the massive belief system reorganization that was taking place.

I cannot pinpoint the exact moment when I stopped believing in the faith that shaped my life. I would compare it to living with a persistent, unrelenting ache, and then one day, suddenly realizing the ache is gone.

I spent five decades trying to impose a primitive, oversimplified view of existence on a very complicated world. Ironically, life became simpler when I let go of my faith-driven perspective, and with a rational mindset, embraced life's complexity.[53]

I felt a huge weight had been lifted from my shoulders, and part of the burden that was removed was the stress of finding, remembering, and sharing answers to the many apparent reasons why faith frequently did not work as advertised.

In my years as a minister, I found that defending some aspects of my theological beliefs required responses so complex, that even after careful study, thinking it through, and determining my own position, with the passing of time I could forget the convoluted answers I had learned.

I was amazed at how questions that had required the mental gymnastics of brain-bending, hard to understand explanations became remarkably easy to answer once I stepped away from faith.

Because of this gradual transformation in my thinking and beliefs, I now have one simple answer to the four questions I've asked in this book:

Christianity—and all other religions—are the creations of human minds, and there is no all-powerful, all-knowing, personal, loving God.

Why does faith in the resurrected, empowered Jesus generate such inconsistent results? Answer: Christianity—and all other religions—are the creations of human minds and there is no all-powerful, all-knowing, personal, loving God.

Faith in Jesus produces inconsistent results because Jesus was a Jewish apocalyptic prophet who is now deceased.

A popular argument used by Christian apologists is that Jesus had to be one of four things: a legend, a liar, a lunatic, or Lord as he claimed to be. The argument goes like this:

> One logical possibility is that Jesus could have been a legend—that he did not actually exist. But the records of the New Testament, references to Jesus by some secular historians, and the existence of Christianity with its eventual explosive growth are strong evidence that Jesus is not a fictional character.

> Another possibility is that Jesus was a liar— someone who knew the claims he made about himself were not true. But the portrayal we have of his character—his compassion for outcasts, his healing of infirmities, his willingness to forgive, his inspiring ethical teachings, and his sacrificial death—is inconsistent with the ability to lie about one's identity.

A third possibility is that Jesus was a lunatic. Mental illness could have prompted Jesus to actually think he was God, although he was an ordinary man. But the New Testament account of his life and ministry does not reveal the symptoms of a person who is mentally ill. His talks and teachings are too coherent. His moral behavior is too consistent. Jesus doesn't look or sound like a lunatic.

The last of the four logical possibilities is that Jesus was, in fact, the Lord, that he was exactly who he said he was—the Son of God who came to take away the sins of the world. The witness of the New Testament, the spiritual intensity displayed in the lives of early Christians, the fact that Christianity has survived and thrived through centuries of dramatic political, scientific, and cultural changes, the impact of Christianity on Western Civilization, and the way his power is displayed in the lives of modern-day believers all point to the truth—Jesus is the Lord of life. He is who he claimed to be.[54]

As a Christian minister, I ate this up. Without hesitation, I accepted that these were the only four options for who Jesus could be, and I bought into the premise that any dialog about Jesus's identity had to be framed around these options. For me, it became a standard line of argument— concise and powerful—in my response to any question about Jesus's claim to be God.

Today, I see this as an inadequate and contrived framework for discussing the identity of Jesus.

Lunatic? Let's agree to use mental illness as the descriptor rather than "lunatic." If you think you're God, but you're not, you're mentally ill regardless of what other symptoms are present or absent. But it makes no sense to pass judgment on whether Jesus was God by looking for symptoms of mental illness when we know him only from ancient books written decades after he lived by authors whose aim was selling the notion that he was the savior of humankind. If he did display symptoms of mental illness, we cannot assume the Gospel writers would have recognized them or written about them if they did.

Liar? Con artists like Bernie Madoff can be remarkably adept at lying without anyone figuring it out, even after decades of personal interactions. The good qualities ascribed to Jesus don't automatically mean he couldn't have one glaring character flaw and be a liar. Still, I don't think Jesus built his ministry on something he knew to be untrue.

Legend? There is now an active movement called mythicism, which offers worthy-of-consideration evidence that Jesus did not exist.[55] I'm not ready to go that far, but I do think the most significant launch point to the next level of examination of Jesus's identity relates to the accuracy of what was written about him.

Some of the information we have about Jesus appears to be factual while other information about him was likely made up by his followers. So, what we seem to have is a combination of reality and legend or what we might describe as augmented reality.

A critical study of the authorship, dates, and content of the Gospels indicates that it's hard to sort out what Jesus thought about himself and what those who followed him said and wrote about his identity after his death.

The Gospels were written by anonymous authors decades after Jesus's death and frequently don't see with the same eyes or speak with the same voice. Their proclamations of the deity of Jesus are most clearly developed and expressed in John's Gospel, which was the last of the four Gospels to be written—some 60 years after the crucifixion.

Church leaders argued about the exact nature of Jesus's deity for centuries after his death until they eventually voted on what became the orthodox view: that Jesus was and is fully God and fully man.

Another suspicious and troubling aspect of the Gospels is what they don't say. Jesus is presented as the only person who ever lived a perfect life, but we have records of his words and actions only for his one to three- year period of ministry. We know about his birth, infancy, and one incident when he was 12 years old, but that's all.

So, why doesn't the Bible provide as much information as

possible about as many years as possible when it comes to the only sinless life that was lived? The answer is simple: Jesus wasn't God, and he didn't live a perfect life.

Jesus might have had an impressive childhood, admirable adolescence, and stellar performance as a young adult, but whatever stories could be drawn from those years were stories of one more imperfect human living and learning from his mistakes. And some would likely be stories of a young man who wasn't yet quite sure what he was supposed to do in life—stories that would have weakened or destroyed THE story.

It's likely that Jesus did exist and that he saw himself as one sent by God to usher in an apocalyptic era when God would judge and reign. But it's not clear that Jesus believed he was God. And it's not a given that Jesus came back to life after his death on the cross.

Issues with the Gospels' account of the resurrection of Jesus were discussed in chapter four, but the most persuasive reason to reject the resurrection claim is visible here and now:

If Jesus were still alive—indwelling and empowering every individual who has believed in him and made a commitment to him—we would see consistent and compelling evidence that the Christian life is supernaturally powered. And it would be clear that Christianity—unlike every other religion—is a way that God lives through human individuals.

But the opposite is true. Despite the impressive and inspirational lives lived by some Christians, faith in Jesus produces inconsistent results because Jesus was a Jewish apocalyptic prophet who is now deceased.

Christian conversion isn't the supernatural experience it claims to be for the same reason. Praying to give your life to Jesus—no matter how sincerely the commitment is made—is a pledge to a man who died centuries ago.

What about the deep emotions many Christians experience when they are "born again?" Conversion is a psychological experience not limited to Christianity. Feeling that something powerful happened to you when you prayed to give your life to Jesus occurs in response to what you've been told should happen, what you've seen happen to other believers, and your desire to have such an experience.

Believing that your God is speaking to you in his still, small voice is in the same category. It's an experience that can be attained in any religion regardless of who or what that religion portrays God to be.

To whatever extent faith—any religious faith—works for an individual or group, it is not for the claimed reasons. Whatever happens in the name of faith is a result of human beliefs and actions, nothing more.

In the church, positive acts and positive feelings are powered by the energy and mutual support of the church's human members, not by any power from God.

For individuals, faith works only to the extent that you work hard at understanding, applying, and living it, and even then, it often doesn't work at all. There's no supernatural power involved.

Any good feelings that result from practicing faith are manufactured in your brain. Some of the actions prompted by faith—like loving, forgiving, and living by the Golden Rule—feel good because we've evolved to live in communities where we depend on one another for our survival.

How could a loving God who created a universe do such a poor job at clearly revealing who he is and what he expects? Answer: Christianity—and all other religions—are the creations of human minds, and there is no all-powerful, all-knowing, personal, loving God.

No God—including the God of the Bible—has clearly and compellingly self-revealed.

If the Bible is God's revelation of himself to humanity, we must conclude that God is either incapable of effective communication or that he thought it would be fun to spend thousands of years watching humans argue and even fight wars over what is true about him.

The Bible makes a thousand times more sense when you view it as a collection of human writings by people who were making up answers to troubling questions about why things happen, attempting to institute rules to maintain order, and trying to help people not feel powerless in the face of struggles, suffering, and death.

The angry God of the Old Testament seems different from the more loving God of the New Testament because God is a fictional character. The God portrayed in the Bible reflects the views of humans who were making up things about a God they needed to believe in, and those perceptions changed over the centuries as life became more civilized.

All the religions in the world become instantly understandable when you see them as human-made. Different people in different cultures created their own explanations for why things are the way they are, who God is, and what he expects.

The number of adherents in a given place follows the history of where the religion started and how the religion's adherents moved into different parts of the world or how missionary work spread the message to new locales.

And childhood indoctrination is an indispensable tool in maintaining a religion for succeeding generations regardless of a new or old location on a map.

If there is a God, he, she, or it is not a self-revealing God.

Imagine creating humans then watching in silence for millenniums as they make up countless stories about you and rules they say came from you. You might chuckle at how ridiculous some of their ideas are—how off-target and untrue—but you say nothing. Eventually, they begin to fight and kill each other over their different beliefs about who you are and what you want from them, but you just watch in silence—never revealing yourself in a clear, compelling way that would end all doubts.

A God who watches in silence and does not provide clear, unambiguous proof of who s/he/it is and what is expected of men and women is not a loving God who wishes to be known.

Why didn't Jesus say anything about germs? Answer: Christianity—and all other religions—are the creations of human minds, and there is no all-powerful, all-knowing, personal, loving God.

Jesus was one more Jewish prophet, a man of his own time who knew no more about microscopic organisms and sanitation procedures than anyone else. He didn't mention germs because he knew nothing about them.

Relief from what would have been hundreds of millions of premature deaths came when science discovered germs and solutions to germs. The lifespan revolution happened in the 20th century, not the first century.

Jesus is not the Great Physician, and we can put the same stock in his reported healings as we do in the miracles done by televangelists today.

And we shouldn't just ask why Jesus was silent on the topic of germs. We must take the query back to the beginning of humanity and ask, "Why did God stand by all those millenniums and watch as those created in his image suffered and died by the hundreds of millions? The answer: There was no personal, loving, all-knowing, and all-powerful God to be watching. There was silence and inaction because such a being does not exist.

Why would a heavenly father condemn most of his children to eternal torment when he could send them all straight to heaven? Answer: Christianity—and all other religions—are the creations of human minds, and there is no all-powerful, all-knowing, personal, loving God.

The biblical story of man's sinfulness and God's plan of redemption doesn't add up because it's made up.

It's a silly plan not just because of the talking snake and a woman made from a man's rib. It's a plan that prompts Catholic parents to baptize babies to protect them from the consequences of original sin. It's a plan that causes evangelical Christian parents to get nervous in those months or years when a child seems old enough to know s/he should accept Jesus and the gift of eternal life but hasn't made that life-altering decision yet. An untimely death could result in an eternity of suffering in hell.

It's a silly plan because the God who claims to want to be known by all people, made it difficult for future missionaries to spread the story of Jesus when he took down the Tower of Babel and supposedly instantly replaced one common human language with many.

It's a silly plan because it promises a perfect life in heaven where there will be no disobedience, and all will be well. But Satan—who once lived in the heavenly presence of God—rebelled and fell hard. So, how do we know something like that couldn't happen again—in God's new heaven.

Speaking of the devil, given that he's wreaking havoc around the world and driving people away from God's plan, isn't it silly that God doesn't simply take Satan out— or better still, redeem him? That would be one heck of a Christian testimonial to advertise for next Sunday's services!

The Bible's plan of redemption is a silly plan because it doesn't make sense that a loving heavenly father would be the author of any scheme that ends with most of the beings created in his image suffering for eternity—with many or perhaps most of them in hell simply because they never had a fair chance to hear or learn how to accept his plan.

Let's move from silly to reality: There is no big plan for everyone. Everything doesn't happen for a reason. Everything happens for a zillion reasons—one reason connecting with another and another with multiple groupings intersecting at a point in time to push or pull in this or that direction.

The idea of sin is not relevant. Sin would require accountability to a personal creator God who has made the rules clear to everyone and has not made failure inevitable.

Personal responsibility? Yes. Accountability to the law of the land, accountability to community, family, friends, and self? Yes.

Shame and guilt before an intimidating God who will throw you into a furnace if you don't follow his plan? No.

We need help in life, but not because we need to be forgiven by a deity.

Life is a battle for survival. Natural catastrophes happen. Even with all the medical advances that have conquered or nearly conquered diseases that have long plagued humanity, sickness is still an inevitable fact of life.

Evil does exist, but it doesn't come from a devil or any other spiritual entity. The pain inflicted by humans on humans comes from multiple sources.

We are evolving animals who sometimes struggle with the more primitive side of our nature. We are gene-survival driven in ways we are only beginning to understand.

Our brains are subject to maladies, and sometimes brains don't work correctly. We can be wounded in our childhood years in ways that cause chronic emotional pain and damage to all our relationships.

Our primitive instincts, survival issues, psychological problems, and emotional wounds can do tremendous harm, sometimes creating situations and events so injurious that we must label them—and sometimes those who cause them—as evil.

We need to help each other in the face of all of life's challenges. Together, we can recover from disasters, find cures for diseases, overcome evil, and help one another in the face of sickness, suffering, and death.

We don't need to worry about eternity. Your brain, with all its capacity to house emotion, memory, personality, creativity, fact, and interpretation, and with all its connections to the various parts of your body, is you. Nothing else—including the concept of a soul—is needed to explain who you are.

Consequently, this life is all we have. There is no afterlife for which we must prepare. As much as we might want some other, better life after this one, there is currently no reliable evidence to support that wish.

Life is to be lived now—today. Today offers countless opportunities. Today we can help each other. Today we can share the joys of life. Today we can grow, smile, build relationships, learn from past mistakes, and make meaningful connections.

The four questions raised in the preceding pages have one simple answer:

Christianity—and all other religions—are the creations of human minds, and there is no all-powerful, all-knowing, personal, loving God.

But how can I assert that my one all-purpose answer is right and true when faith seems to work so well for so many people?

6 – The Way Faith Works

What follows is a parable that explains how faith works. It's a story about a man named Dan and a miraculous device called the Amazing Disk.

All Dan's friends are talking about the Amazing Disk—known as A.D. for short. The press is proclaiming A.D. as the world's greatest electronic device, and social media is singing its praises on every available platform.

Why? You can ask the Amazing Disk for anything—whatever you want. Just ask, and you will receive.

Remarkably, the A.D. isn't very expensive. Priced at a mere $99, not only is it affordable, but it's extremely simple to use. When Dan's A.D. is delivered at his door, he eagerly opens the UPS box, unpacks the new gadget, and delights in its thin, circular shape, small enough to slip into a pocket.

The QuickStart instructions couldn't be more straightforward: "The Amazing Disk will assist you when you tell it what you need. You can ask it for anything. It is guaranteed to work, 100% of the time. Install one AAA battery, push the power button, wait for the two indicator lights to come on, and ask for what you need."

Dan unwraps the AAA battery that comes with the A.D. and pops it into the device. Then he pushes the power button, and the two LEDs light up immediately—one green, indicating the device is on, and the other blue, indicating the A.D. is connected to its global network. Dan's A.D. is ready to use.

Excitedly, Dan makes his first request. "Help me to have a good day at work tomorrow." The A.D. doesn't respond. It doesn't talk back. It doesn't blink its lights. It doesn't do anything. It isn't supposed to.

The next morning, Dan goes to work filled with anticipation. It's a Friday, and sure enough, he has a fantastic day. When he gets home, he feels a little embarrassed, but he leans down toward the A.D. and earnestly says, "Thank you."

On Saturday morning, Dan makes another request to the Amazing Disk. "Please help my wife and me to have some quality relationship time today." That afternoon, Dan and his wife, Leslie, pack a picnic basket and take a short drive to the countryside, where they find a beautiful secluded spot. There, they spread out a blanket, and enjoy a bottle of Merlot and a delicious evening meal. After eating, they chat and laugh together like they used to, but haven't done in years. They cozy up for a little kissing as the sun goes down, then head home to a very romantic night. Before he falls asleep, Dan thinks to himself, "The Amazing Disk is incredible!"

The following Monday, Dan decides to give the A.D. a tougher task. He has been expecting his annual bonus at work. Just before he enters his office, he whispers into the disk and says, "I want my bonus to be twice as much as it was last year." The A.D.—once again—does not beep, blink, or respond in any way, but Dan has a good feeling about what is to come.

Unfortunately, when Dan opens the bonus envelope, he finds that his check is less than the previous year. He is sorely disappointed, and immediately wonders, "Did I make my Amazing Disk request properly?"

Remembering his A.D. came with a 1,156-page user's manual, at the end of the day, Dan settles himself into his favorite chair and pores over the Frequently Asked Questions section. Noting that the FAQ is extremely long, he is pleased to see that the issue he is inquiring about is first in the list. It reads: "I asked the Amazing Disk for something and did not receive it." A multi-step problem-solving routine follows.

> **Step 1:** Did you really believe the Amazing Disk would provide what you requested? The Amazing Disk analyzes subtle cues in your voice that enable it to discern your level of belief that your request will be granted. The next time you ask the Amazing Disk for

something, make sure you truly believe that
what you are asking for will happen. If you
have already done this and it did not resolve
the issue, go to **Step 2**.

Armed with an improved understanding of how to make
his request, Dan decides to put the disk to the test once
more. Before telling the device what he wants, he focuses
on cranking up as much belief as possible. He repeats his
request for a larger bonus—this time filled with faith: "I
would like my boss to come into my office today, tell me
there was a mistake in calculating my bonus, then hand me
a new check that is double last year's amount." Hopeful
and determined, Dan goes to work. But at the end of the
day, there is no visit from the boss and no revised bonus.

Unwilling to give up, that evening, Dan sits back down in
his living room chair with the user's manual. Under the
issue labeled "I asked the Amazing Disk for something and
did not receive it" he reads **Step 2**—the next step if **Step 1**
didn't work.

Step 2: If you truly believed the Amazing Disk
would provide what you requested and did not
receive it, try making the same request every
day for 30 days. If you have already done this
and it did not resolve the issue, go to **Step 3**.

Relieved to find a way to tweak his request, Dan knows he
just has to follow the directions. So, every day for the next
30 days, he pushes himself to a high level of belief and

makes the same request: that his boss would walk in with a replacement bonus check that doubles last year's amount. On the 31st day, he is disappointed again. There is still no new bonus. Discouraged, but not one to give up easily, Dan returns to the user's manual and reads **Step 3**.

> **Step 3**: If you truly believed the Amazing Disk would provide what you requested and made the request every day for 30 days but still did not receive it, try carrying the Amazing Disk with you throughout the day and make your request multiple times each day. If you have already done this and it did not resolve the issue, go to **Step 4**.

For the next month, the Amazing Disk is always in Dan's pocket. He is on a crusade—working to keep his A.D. belief level high at all times, and making his big bonus request not once, but 10 times daily for another 30 days. To his dismay, the result is the same—no new bonus.

Dan returns to the user's manual, steeling himself for **Step 4**.

> **Step 4**: If you truly believed the Amazing Disk would provide what you requested and carried the Amazing Disk on your person making the request multiple times a day for 30 days, but still did not receive your request, ask at least four of your friends to make the request with you using their Amazing Disks. Requests

made by multiple users are more powerful than requests made by one user. If you have already done this and it did not resolve the issue, go to **Step 5**.

Dan is delighted. Surely this will work. He considers himself lucky to have four friends who are also A-Diskers—the moniker for avid A.D. users—and once he explains his situation, all four agree to ask the A.D. for Dan's boss to walk into his office with a new bonus check that would bring the year's total to twice as large as last year's. All four also agree to meet the necessary conditions: maintaining a high belief level, carrying the Amazing Disk wherever they go, and repeating the request multiple times a day for the next month.

But after the month passes, Dan still has no new bonus. Discouraged, but determined to pursue all recommended solutions, and buoyed by his A-Disker friends, he returns to the user's manual, **Step 5**.

> **Step 5**: If you truly believed the Amazing Disk would provide what you requested, and carried the Amazing Disk on your person making the request multiple times a day for 30 days with at least four other Amazing Disk users joining you in all these actions, but still did not receive what you requested, this most likely means that the Amazing Disk has determined that providing what you requested would not be in your long-term best interest.

It may be hard to understand this right now but exercise the same confidence you had in the Amazing Disk when making your initial request to believe that not getting what you asked for is actually what is best for you. Work on being grateful that you did not get what you asked for because this is a sign that the Amazing Disk is looking out for you at a level that is currently beyond your understanding. Trusting the wisdom of the Amazing Disk even when it does not give you what you want will increase the likelihood of having your requests granted in the future. The more you use the Amazing Disk, the more you will understand that simply talking to the Amazing Disk may be just as meaningful as having it give you the things you think you need.

Under **Step 5** is a note.

Note: Some requests may be outside the scope of what the Amazing Disk is designed to do. Keep this in mind when deciding what types of requests to make to the Amazing Disk in the future. Always remember, your relationship with the Amazing Disk is more important than whether it says yes to all the things you request.

Dan concludes that the A.D. is telling him that he needs something more important than a bigger bonus; he needs more patience and more gratitude for all the good in his life.

Over time, Dan makes other requests and often receives exactly what he requests. But he notices that the Amazing Disk seems best for answering requests that involve outcomes over which he exercises a lot of control, outcomes that might have happened anyway, and outcomes that could be interpreted as either positive or negative depending on how he looks at it.

Feeling somewhat skeptical, but wanting to keep believing in the A.D., Dan calls the Amazing Disk support line. A cheerful woman—definitely an A-Disker—answers. Dan explains that while many of his A.D. requests have been granted, some of his more important requests have received no response though he has attempted to follow all the instructions in the user's manual. Admitting that he was overwhelmed by the size and complexity of the 1,156-page manual, he asks if there is any other help available. The A.D. staffer replies, "You should enroll in our three-month A-Disker course, 'How to Talk to Your Amazing Disk.'"

With the staffer's help, Dan signs up for the very next training session offered at a nearby A.D. Training Center. He attends the class each week for three months and enjoys sitting in a circle with 11 other A-Diskers—both sharing his own A.D. requests and listening to the requests made by the other group members. Dan feels cared for by the other A-Diskers—even when the disk does not give him what he requests.

After completing the three-month class, Dan signs up for the next level and attends for another six months, then the advanced class, which lasts 12 months. In the advanced class, two members of the group knew someone who knew someone who knew someone who had experienced actual miracles in response to their A.D. requests. Dan was impressed.

After completing the advanced class, Dan starts attending ongoing weekly A-Disker sessions. He now understands that learning how to talk to the A.D. is a lifelong process.

He has also learned that the A.D. does not make mistakes—if something doesn't seem to be working, it isn't the A.D. underperforming, but rather, he is failing in some manner—most likely a lack of belief or a lack of patience or a lack of humility on his part.

Dan never attempted to take the A.D. apart and look inside, but had he done so, he would have found only a few wires connecting the parts visible on the outside—the power switch, the green light, and the blue light—to the battery. There were no sophisticated internal electronics connecting the A.D. to a network of any kind.

For Dan, what was inside the A.D. was irrelevant. What was important—living in daily dialogue with the A.D. and other A-Diskers. That was all he really needed.[56]

7 – The Exits Are Blocked

Why is it so hard to leave your faith even when you don't really believe it anymore? After I finally walked away from faith, I asked myself why I had stayed so long. How could I keep my eyes closed for decades to such evident fatal flaws in my beliefs?

Part of the story may be genetic. We may have evolved to favor a less risky position on faith—a sort of "better safe than sorry" approach that is about survival.

Imagine a primitive man walking alone across a field. He hears a noise behind him. What is it? It could be a wild animal about to pounce, or it could be the rustling of the wind. If he assumes the noise is danger and responds in a way to defend himself, he's more likely to survive, whatever the source of the noise. If he doesn't prepare for the worst and assumes it's just a gust, he is at greater risk of being killed.

Those who respond to the possibility of danger, whether it exists or not, are more likely to survive, and thus to pass their genes along—including this trait.[57]

The relevance to contemporary Christianity? If there might be a hell, then assume the danger exists and take evasive action—embrace faith. It's called Pascal's Wager: If you're betting on eternity with your life, act as if God exists, because you have less to lose if you're wrong.

Even if we accept the hypothesis of a genetic component, faith is about much more. Once established, faith plants deep roots. A broken belief system is hard to leave, especially when learned during formative childhood years. Its inconsistencies are easy to tolerate when faith provides meaning, security, and hope—all of which are tough to abandon when you are linked to a community that keeps reminding you: "You are one of us. You are not one of them. We are okay. They are not okay. Leaving us would be the worst thing you could ever do."

If we cannot make some sense of life, we may be tempted to give up. To keep going, we may opt for a set of not-so-good reasons for seeing life as meaningful over no reasons at all. In other words, inaccurate or far-fetched beliefs are better than hopelessness. Our need to make sense of things is so strong that we may hold onto to a flawed belief system even after we have seen its deficiencies repeatedly. This was what I did.

Once you commit to living your life as a person of faith—once you start the journey—faith becomes a part of you that is hard to jettison. We may think of the faith journey like climbing the world's highest peak and looking for anything that will help along the way, as illustrated in the following parable.

Frank is about to climb Mount Everest and knows he is risking his life to do so. On the way to base camp, he stops to pray at a remote temple where he meets a monk. With an air of mysticism, the monk convincingly predicts that Frank will make it to the summit and descend safely, but warns, "There is one thing you must do. You must wear this magic coat I am giving you. There is no other coat like it. This coat will not only keep you warm, but it will also empower you to make it to the top and back down the mountain. It will give you courage, endurance, and protection. Only with this coat will you succeed. Without it, you will surely die on the mountain."

Frank is mesmerized by the words of the monk. He leaves a generous offering and dons the one-of-a-kind magic coat—a coat that looks like any other but has hidden powers.

Soon, Frank is trudging upward with other climbers, one of whom is wearing a coat just like his. The climber asks Frank where he got his coat and upon learning it was from the monk, laughs and asks, "How much did you give him for your magic coat?"

The laughing climber explains that the man is not a monk but a shrewd salesman who has learned that he gets paid the most for a coat when he boasts of its powers, gives it away and asks for nothing in return. He tells Frank that a number of the climbers who donned the monk imposter's magic coats have frozen to death on the mountain.

Successfully climbing the world's highest peak is not about wearing a magic garment. It's about conditioning, timing, good decisions, endurance, and luck—but you do need protection from the cold.

As much as Frank wants to take off the coat and fling it into the nearest crevasse, he has no other coat to wear. No matter how much the coat reminds him of his gullibility, he needs it to survive the chill of the wind. He doesn't need the coat to be magic—he just needs it to keep him warm. Without the coat, he will die. He doesn't stop wearing the coat because it's all he has.

Once faith becomes the way you cope with challenges, pain, and problems, once a community of faith becomes your support system, and once you have disavowed all other avenues for finding meaning, it's hard to disconnect. It's hard to take off the coat.

Proofs of the illogical nature of faith, arguments that science makes more sense than religion, and the idea that a true God would reveal himself more clearly and precisely simply do not matter. None of these arguments will likely sway you when you continue to feel that faith is enabling you to keep moving ahead toward your goals.

When a warm sense of hope, comfort, and community have been provided, it is hard even to consider removing the magic coat of faith. In this context, the fear of feeling disheartened or alone can easily triumph over logical thinking, and it may seem that all exits from the magical thinking that characterizes faith are blocked.[58]

My theory is that a believer can't be objective until there's some bruising collision with reality that is emotionally jarring, something that loosens up the thought process.

Life events pushed me out onto the diving board of disbelief. It took years for me to inch my way to the end of that diving board and take the long plunge into a skeptical, rational, and reasoned approach to the world.

Soon I felt lighter, and truth felt more accessible. And I felt more freedom than ever before. But leaving faith also made me feel angry, ashamed, and profoundly sad.

I felt angry at the religious system that pulled me in when I was a child and robbed me of a more rational process of selecting my vocation. I felt angry at myself for leading others down the same path. I felt angry at the seductive shallowness of what I believed—simple answers that faith taught me never to question, answers that didn't address life's complexity.

I felt ashamed of how easy it is to see the truth once you are willing. How could I have been so blind? How could I have gone for so many years convinced of so many things that are so obviously illogical and untrue?

And yet I missed the warmth of Christian fellowship that

feels like forever but vanishes in the wind when you walk away from it. I was profoundly sad in my awareness that I no longer had a tribe.[59]

I know how good life in church can feel. I understand the sense of community and shared purpose. I know what it's like to join in heartfelt singing with a thousand members of your spiritual family on a Sunday morning.

I've seen over and over how Christians share support and comfort when a death or other tragedy strikes. And I remember the Christmas Eve services when we all lit candles that filled the room with a warm glow symbolic of what we felt inside.

I get it. I understand the richness of a deeply committed life.

But what if, right now, I could swallow a pill that would bring my old faith back? Would I do it? Would I take the pill? The answer is no because what I believed is not true, and I found myself unable to pretend.[60]

I wouldn't go back if I could, but I'm wondering if you will move forward. I'm wondering if, like me, you've been jostled by life events that have made you question your faith, and perhaps led you to read this book.

I understand that there are so many motivators prompting you to remain in the path you've always followed. In the cafeteria line of life, it's easy to get into a habit of saying:

"I'll have the eyes-closed, my-tribe-knows-best, don't-want-to-look-at-the-evidence casserole. And for dessert, I'll have the everything-is-the-way-I've-always-understood-it pie."[61]

I can understand why you would want to keep believing in life after death. I can understand if you don't want to lose your spiritual family. And I won't think you're stupid or crazy if—after reading this book—you decide to continue in your faith.

But one thing I've attempted to share with you in these final pages is a vision of what it feels like to break a spell cast long ago, to wake up from a trance, and to experience the freedom to follow the truth wherever it leads.

When I took the plunge off the diving board of disbelief, I soon found the new waters to be clear, cleansing, and refreshing. I was released from believing in a system that does not make sense, and ironically, I became more able to understand, love, and accept humanity in a fundamentally "more Christian" way.[62]

Walking away was not pain-free, but I feel peace in having left faith, church, and religion behind. I never worry that I have made a fatal mistake by changing what I think and believe. I never wonder if hell might be real.

Instead, in my new life beyond faith, the primary question has become "What is true?"[63] and the primary focus is on making the most of this life on earth.

8 – The New Old Me

My Christian belief system taught me that without Jesus leading my life, I would be lost, depraved, living in darkness, and a lover of evil. When I left my faith, I did become less judgmental of others and myself, and I did eventually question, test, and change some facets of my former value system, but I didn't succumb to depravity, darkness, or evil.

My personality did not change. My penchant for direct and honest communication did not go away. My insatiable curiosity has not vanished. I didn't suddenly lose skills or experience or knowledge when I left my faith.

I can still be too intense, too certain I am right, and too quick to feel emotionally hurt, but I still have a willingness to scrutinize my own actions, to take responsibility, and to apologize when I am wrong.

My value system is more the same than different. I did not: stop loving my family and friends, lose interest in the greater good, stop caring about the truth, become insensitive to the needs of others, or stop wanting to be a better person.

I have thought a great deal about how I came to be who I am. Did I become a "good" person simply because of my years of exposure to the church, the Bible, and other Christians? Did I use Christianity to get pointed in the right direction, then abandon it while still benefiting from what it taught me?

The Bible did instruct me to treat other people the way I want to be treated. The Bible did teach me to regard every person the same way, regardless of appearance or social status. My faith taught me to forgive. It encouraged me to be sensitive to the needs of others.

However, I witnessed many people exposed to the same teachings with marginal changes in their lives. In 12-Step groups, they say, "It works when you work it." In other words, *you* must work it, and Christianity is no different.

I now understand that my Christian faith worked in harmony with some part of me that was eager to please, ready to obey and wanting to excel at goodness. I worked it, and it worked for me for a long time—until I was willing to pull back the wizard's curtain and see what was there and what wasn't.

After I stopped believing, the me who cared about reaching for what is highest and best in myself—and hoping for it in others—was still present.

My faith made me a better person, but my desire to grow was a key factor as well. When I outgrew my faith, I did not lose my desire to grow.

Ironically, after my loss of religious belief—after gaining a new sense of bearing—I had a strong sense that I was becoming the very best version of myself. This has proved to be anything but a fleeting sensation. I continue to feel myself to be more authentic and genuinely transparent. I have been able to give other people more room to be whoever they chose to be, and that includes religious choices.

I also feel a sense of relief as if a heavy weight has been lifted off my shoulders—a result of no longer presuming to hear the voice of God, resigning from the defense team for a silent deity, accepting how much I do not know, and ending the mental gymnastics required by faith.[64]

In a note to a friend not long after I had left my faith, I wrote:

> Despite the changes in my beliefs, I love life with all its mystery and complexity. There are so many unanswered questions, so much to discover. Humans are capable of great evil, but also great good. For me, this life, the here and now of it, is more important than ever, and not one day should be wasted.[65]

Today, I choose to live a value-driven life, to embrace life's ups and downs, to seek purpose and significance, and to find meaning and joy in the process. This is the new me, yet also the me that has always been here, but is now freed to follow the truth and hopefully to create new avenues for personal growth in the lives of others.[66]

If you're interested in the full story of my life journey into and out of faith, you can read about it in *Goodbye Jesus: An Evangelical Preacher's Journey Beyond Faith.*

After thinking carefully about how my post-faith life would look, I decided that if I could share a religion-not-required way of pursuing meaning in life, it would be something worth sharing. I wanted to describe a value-driven, purpose-oriented lifestyle that could work for anyone—regardless of religious beliefs, political stance, personality type, lifestyle, or generational label. So, after completing *Goodbye Jesus*, I wrote a follow-up book titled *How to Live a Meaningful Life: Focusing on Things that Matter.*

At the core of my new meaning-driven lifestyle is a new mantra for day-to-day living:

Dig deep, aim high, and find your best self in the present moment. Connect.[67]

Feedback Invited

I am wondering how you have reacted to what you have read in the preceding pages, and I would like to invite you to share your response. Thanks to Amazon.com, you can provide feedback.

You will need to decide how many stars to give my book, and, of course, that's your call. You can stop there, or you can add a short review. I hope you will add some comments to your rating. And I think some of the things I'm interested in knowing will also be meaningful to others who are deciding whether they should read this book.

I'm interested in knowing something about who you are in terms of faith or lack of it, how this book affected you—emotionally, intellectually, spiritually—and whether anything you think about God, faith, or religion has been challenged, shaken, changed, or maybe, reinforced by what I have written. Perhaps you don't agree with anything I now believe, but you learned something about faith, evangelical Christianity, the church, or yourself from my story. That would be helpful to know.

If you too have walked away from faith, and this book made you feel less isolated in your unbelief, I would be encouraged by knowing that.

To add your rating and comments, go to www.Amazon.com, type Tim Sledge in the search box, and press Enter. Find this book in the list, then click on the image of the book. On the book's page, find and click on the customer reviews link, which is just to the right of the star rating for the book. When the customer reviews page opens, click the "Write a Customer Review" button. A new page will open. Click on the number of stars you want to give the book. You can stop there, or you can add some comments. Even one short sentence could be helpful to prospective readers.

Thank you in advance for your response.

You can contact me on my website, MovingTruths.com, where I regularly share insights for personal growth.

You can also follow me on Twitter: https://twitter.com/Goodbye_Jesus.

Suggested Reading

Richard Carrier, *On the Historicity of Jesus: Why We Might Have Reason to Doubt*, (Sheffield, England: Sheffield Phoenix Press, 2014).

Bart D. Ehrman, *How Jesus Became God: The Exaltation of a Jewish Preacher from Galilee* (New York: HarperOne, 2014).

Bart Ehrman, *Lost Christianities: The Battles for Scripture and the Faiths We Never Knew* (New York: Oxford University Press, 2003).

Yuval Noah Harari, *Sapiens: A Brief History of Humankind* (New York: Harper, 2015).

Steven Pinker, *Enlightenment Now: The Case for Reason, Science, Humanism, and Progress* (New York: Penguin Books, 2019).

Michael Shermer, *The Believing Brain* (New York: Henry Holt and Company, 2011).

Phil Zuckerman, *Living the Secular Life* (New York: Penguin Press, 2014).

Endnotes

[1] Matthew 13:1-8, 18-23.

[2] "LifeWay Research: Americans Are Fond of the Bible, Don't Actually Read It," *LifeWay Research*, April 25, 2017, //lifewayresearch.com/2017/04/25/lifeway-research-americans-are-fond-of-the-bible-dont-actually-read-it.

[3] Matthew 28:19-20.

[4] 1 John 4:8.

[5] Tim Sledge, *Goodbye Jesus: An Evangelical Preacher's Journey Beyond Faith* (Houston: Insighting Growth Publications, 2018, Second Edition), 400. Used with Permission. All Rights Reserved Worldwide.

[6] Michael Lipka, "Millennials increasingly are driving growth of 'nones'," Pew Research Center, Washington, D.C., (May 12, 2015), //www.pewresearch.org/ fact-tank/2015/05/12/millennials-increasingly-are-driving-growth-of-nones/, cited in *Goodbye Jesus*, 400.

[7] Tim Sledge, *Goodbye Jesus*, 400-401.

[8] Tim Sledge, *Goodbye Jesus*, 392-393.

[9] Yuval Noah Harari, *Sapiens: A Brief History of Humankind*, (New York: Harper, 2015), 21, 37.

[10] "Germ Theory of Disease," Wikipedia, //en.wikipedia.org/wiki/Germ_theory_of_disease, (accessed July 14,2019).

[11] O.L. Bettmann, *The good old days—they were terrible!*, (New

York: Random House, 1974) and J. Norberg, *Progress: Ten reasons to look forward to the future,* (London: Oneworld, 2016), cited in Steven Pinker, *Enlightenment Now: The Case for Reason, Science, Humanism, and Progress*, (New York: Penguin Books, 2019), 63.

[12] Note: Rounded 32.5 years. Steven Pinker, *Enlightenment Now: The Case for Reason, Science, Humanism, and Progress*, (New York: Penguin Books, 2019), 53.

[13] Harari, 42, 51-52.

[14] Saugat Adhikari, "Top 10 Epidemic Diseases That Were Common in the Ancient World," Ancient History Lists, //www.ancienthistorylists.com/ancient-civilizations/top-10-epidemic-diseases-that-were-common-in-ancient-world, (March 25,2019).

[15] Saugat Adhikari.

[16] Saugat Adhikari.

[17] Saugat Adhikari.

[18] Judith Summers, *Soho: A History of London's Most Colourful Neighborhood*, (London: Bloomsbury Publishing Plc., 1989), 114-116.

[19] "Attempts to prevent illness and disease: Developments in bacteriology: Louis Pasteur and Robert Koch," BBC, //www.bbc.com/bitesize/guides/zq8xk2p/revision/5, (accessed July 14, 2019).

[20] Frederick F. Cartwright, "Joseph Lister: British Surgeon and Medical Scientist," *Encyclopedia Britannica*, //www.britannica.com/biography/Joseph-Lister-Baron-Lister-of-Lyme-Regis, (updated May 7, 2019).

[21] "Brought To Life: Robert Koch (1843-1910)," Science Museum, //broughttolife.sciencemuseum.org.uk/broughttolife/people/robertkoch, (accessed July 14, 2019).

[22] Agnes Ullmann, "Louis Pasteur: French Chemist and Microbiologist: Vaccine Development," *Encyclopedia Britannica*,

//www.britannica.com/biography/Louis-Pasteur/Vaccine-development, (updated July 4, 2019).

[23] Agnes Ullmann.

[24] Josh Martinez, "History of the Cholera Vaccine," Passport Health, //www.passporthealthusa.com/2017/11/history-of-the-cholera-vaccine/, (November 16, 2017).

[25] Yolanda Smith, "Typhoid Fever History," News-Medical.Net, //www.news-medical.net/health/Typhoid-Fever-History.aspx, (accessed July 14, 2019).

[26] "Timeline of Vaccines," Wikipedia, //en.wikipedia.org/wiki/Timeline_of_vaccines, (accessed June 14, 2019).

[27] "History of Drinking Water Treatment: A Century of U.S. Water Chlorination and Treatment: One of the Ten Greatest Public Health Achievements of the 20th Century," Centers for Disease Control and Prevention, //www.cdc.gov/healthywater/drinking/history.html, (November 26, 2012).

[28] "Timeline of Vaccines."

[29] "American Chemical Society International Historic Chemical Landmarks. Discovery and Development of Penicillin," American Chemical Society, //www.acs.org/content/acs/en/education/whatischemistry/landmarks/flemingpenicillin.html (accessed July 14, 2019).

[30] Steven Pinker, 63.

[31] Steven Pinker, 53.

[32] Max Roser, "Life Expectancy: Chart: Life expectancy globally and by world regions since 1770," Our World in Data, //ourworldindata.org/life-expectancy, (accessed July 12, 2019).

[33] Mark 7:1-5.

[34] Mark 7:15.

[35] Bart Ehrman, *Lost Christianities: The Battles for Scripture and the*

Faiths We Never Knew, (New York: Oxford University Press, 2003), 2.

[36] Note: I'm using "orthodox Christianity" in the sense of right belief not as a reference to the Greek Orthodox Church.

[37] Genesis 2:16-17.

[38] Note: Science provides a different view of why women experience so much pain in childbirth: Human babies have big brains and consequently, large heads. In addition, walking upright requires narrower hips which constricts the birth canal. Harari, 10.

[39] Hell has been traditionally seen as a place of fire, but some modern Christians water it down to simply mean unending separation from God and a few see it as being extinguished—not existing any more.

[40] John 1:29.

[41] Romans 5:15.

[42] Luke 2:52.

[43] There are ancient writings outside the Bible that make assertions about things said and done by Jesus prior to his years of ministry, but none of these writings are accepted as authentic by mainstream Christianity.

[44] The Gospel records are not clear on exactly how long the public ministry of Jesus lasted.

[45] Tim Sledge, *Goodbye Jesus*, 390.

[46] Matthew 27:46.

[47] M.G. Harris, Oxford, United Kingdom, Twitter @RealMGHarris, July 19, 2019.

[48] Tim Sledge, *Goodbye Jesus*, 377-378.

[49] Tim Sledge, *Goodbye Jesus*, 379-380.

[50] Tim Sledge, *Goodbye Jesus*, 380-381.

[51] Note: If liberal Christians are correct in asserting that the God of the Bible would never send most of the humans he created to burn in hell for eternity, why did it take almost 2,000 years for Christians to figure

this out?

[52] 1 Peter 3:15.

[53] Tim Sledge, *Goodbye Jesus*, 353-354.

[54] Josh McDowell advocated this defense of faith in a chapter titled: "The Trilemma: Lord, Liar, or Lunatic" in *Evidence that Demands a Verdict: Historical Evidences for the Christian Faith*, (Arrowhead Springs, California: Campus Crusade for Christ, 1972).

[55] Richard Carrier, *On the Historicity of Jesus: Why We Might Have Reason to Doubt*, (Sheffield, England: Sheffield Phoenix Press, 2014).

[56] Tim Sledge, "Faith Games," *Goodbye Jesus*, 404-408.

[57] Michael Shermer, *The Believing Brain* (New York: Henry Holt and Company, 2011), 59.

[58] Tim Sledge, *Goodbye Jesus*, 360-361.

[59] Tim Sledge, *Goodbye Jesus*, 362-363.

[60] Tim Sledge, *Goodbye Jesus*, 363.

[61] Tim Sledge, *A Meta-Spiritual Handbook: How to Be Spiritual without Religion, Faith, or God,* (Houston: Insighting Growth Publications, *2018),* 20.

[62] Tim Sledge, *Goodbye Jesus*, 363.

[63] Tim Sledge, *Goodbye Jesus*, 417.

[64] Tim Sledge, *Goodbye Jesus*, 409-410.

[65] Tim Sledge, *Goodbye Jesus*, 410.

[66] Tim Sledge, *Goodbye Jesus*, 416.

[67] Tim Sledge, *How to Live a Meaningful Life: Focusing on Things that Matter*, 153.

Printed in Great Britain
by Amazon

38399471R00078